ALPHABET FUN & GAMES

Activities and Game Sheets for Teaching the Alphabet

Jill M. Coudron

MAKEMASTER® Blackline Masters

Fearon Teacher Aids
a division of
PITMAN LEARNING, INC.
Belmont, California

Editorial director: Ina Tabibian
Editor: Robin Kelly
Illustrator: Susan True
Design director: Eleanor Mennick
Production editor: Anne Lewis
Manufacturing director: Susan Siegel

ISBN-0-8224-0295-5
Library of Congress Catalog Card Number: 83-62563
Printed in the United States of America.
1.98765432

PREFACE

Alphabet Fun and Games is the fourth title in Jill Coudron's delightful series of alphabet activity books. Three earlier companion books include *Alphabet Puppets*, *Alphabet Stories*, and *Alphabet Activities*. Together, the ideas and reproducible materials in these four books will enable you to teach letter recognition and sounds through meaningful learning experiences in all curricular areas.

Alphabet Puppets introduces the idea of teaching the alphabet through puppets accompanied by stories, songs, cooking projects, and other varied learning activities. It provides patterns for making the puppets as well as ideas for incorporating the alphabet program into your classroom. It presents an effective method of teaching the alphabet that is stimulating for both the teacher and the child.

In *Alphabet Stories*, the puppets experience special adventures, which are pictorially portrayed. The letters and the sounds are carefully interwoven through the stories. Reproducible pages enable children to share the stories and puppet caricatures with their families, extending the learning beyond the classroom into the home.

Alphabet Activities presents additional learning activities, which broaden the concepts introduced in *Alphabet Puppets*. It contains many new ideas for all curricular areas, simple cooking projects in which children are actively involved, and two reproducible activity pages for each letter. A wide range of activities is available to facilitate different teaching and learning styles. Incorporated, too, are ideas that enable teachers to work with children individually, in small groups, and as a class.

Alphabet Fun and Games features just what the title promises—lots of fun and games. For each letter of the alphabet there is a section of creative movement activities, structured games for classes or groups, a snack recipe with additional tasting suggestions, poems and songs with accompanying movements, and two pages of reproducible material for constructing a game. A special art page displays a finger alphabet you can teach your children.

CONTENTS

INTRODUCTION

Alphabet Fun and Games is a collection of activities designed to help children learn the alphabet and its sounds. It can be used for preschool, kindergarten, and early-grade children as well as for learning-disabled students. Included for each letter of the alphabet are sections featuring creative movement, games, snacks, and songs and poems with accompanying movements. In addition, there are two reproducible pages for each letter that will enable you to make a classroom game to use with a small group of children.

Scope of Activities

The activities in this book are intended to help prepare children to be successful learners in an atmosphere of fun and enjoyment. The activities encompass early learning experiences in the areas of visual discrimination, visual memory, language and vocabulary development, visual motor coordination, and fine and large motor control. Each activity operates around one letter and its sound.

How to Use the Games

The games on the reproducible pages of this book are intended to be played with small groups of children. Use them as a reinforcement of skills presented. Teach the appropriate letter game during the week of that letter and make it available after that week for the children to use during their free time.

As you prepare the games, make them more long-lasting by laminating each gameboard or covering it with clear contact paper after you have colored and decorated it. Some of the games will fit nicely in file folders. The game pieces that accompany them can be stored in clear plastic bags attached to the folders. Store other games in attractive, sturdy boxes. Prepare an area of your room to keep the games. They should be accessible to the children. A box decorated with pretty contact paper can hold the folder games.

Adapt the games if the skills presented in the book are inappropriate for your children. Cover the words, letters, or numbers you want changed, using paper labeled with your substitute material. Reproduce the game sheets after the changes have been made.

Some of the games require markers or counters. Use anything you have available, such as small toys, cars, blocks, or buttons.

Finger Alphabet

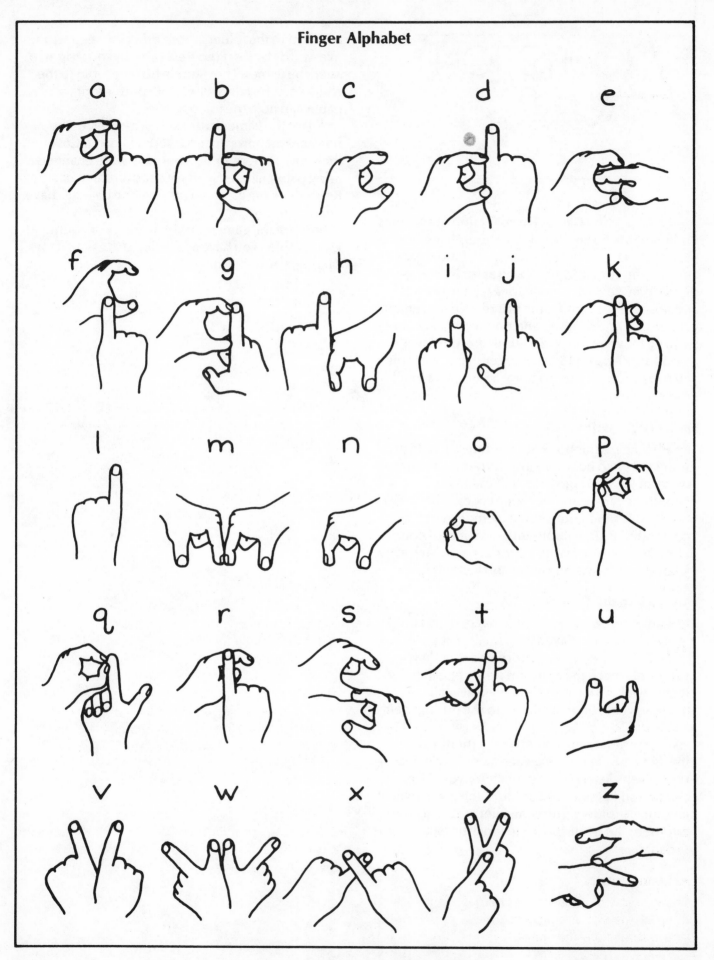

MOVEMENTS

Alligator Swamp

Give each child a jump rope or piece of string. Ask the children to lay it out on the floor in a circular shape to represent an alligator swamp. Direct them to move around it with different movements you call out: walking, skipping, hopping, galloping, and so on. Ask them to jump in and out of the swamp without touching the rope.

Airplanes

Ask the children to pretend to be flying airplanes. Let them move quickly around the play area with their arms extended. Call out directions as they "fly," then ask the "airplanes" to land. Let all the airplanes stand on a line and listen as you call out different colors. Only those airplanes wearing the color you call may take off and fly around. If your class knows how to read color words, hold up flash cards with color names and ask them to fly, only if their color comes up on one of the cards.

Ants

Lay out a large blanket. Ask children to get down on their hands and knees and crawl like little ants on a picnic blanket. Call out movements such as forward, backward, to the left, to the right, fast, slow, and so on.

Air Ball

Find a very large, lightweight ball. Show it to the children and ask them what is inside. Let the children take turns throwing it up as high as they can and catching it. Divide the class into small groups or pairs to continue the activity.

Alligator Crawl

Show the children how to crawl like alligators. Have them lay flat on their stomachs and use bent arms and legs to scoot along the floor.

Astronauts

Show the children a picture of an astronaut and talk about what an astronaut might do on the job. Let the children pretend to be astronauts . Ask them to "blast off" and run, hop, skip, or walk around a large play area. Let them pretend to land on the moon and walk as if there is no gravity. To end this activity, ask children to lay flat on their backs on the floor and pretend to hold on tightly to the spaceship as it lands back on Earth.

Alphabet Actions

Ask the children to mirror your actions as you say the alphabet. Make a different motion as you name each letter. Examples might be bending over and touching toes, stretching tall, jumping, holding up arms or legs, and so on.

Apples

Ask the children to pretend to be apples on a tree. Play musical scales on a piano or xylophone for them to move to as they "fall" down. Vary the tempo of the falling. Ask the children to roll on the floor as an apple might roll on the ground.

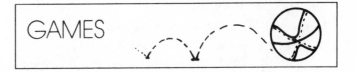

GAMES

Animal Name Game

Ask the children to form a circle with their hands joined. Choose a leader to stand outside the circle. The inside of the circle represents the forest. Repeating four or five animal names in consecutive order, assign each player in the circle a particular animal. Place one of each type of animal in the forest. The leader calls out the name of one of the animals. The children around the circle who have been assigned that animal must change places. The child in the center with that animal name tries to get a place. Change leaders often.

Animal Acting

Let the children dramatize different movements of the animals that you name. Ask each child to choose an animal for everyone to act out. Make it a guessing game.

3

ALPHABET SNACK

"Apricats"

Serve each child two canned apricot halves. Show them how to put the apricots together on a plate, forming the head and body of a cat. Provide cut-up dried apricots to form the ears and tail. Let the children make faces on the heads and a letter **A** on the bodies of the "apricats." Provide raisins, chow mein noodles (for whiskers), or other chopped fruit or nuts. Discuss the taste difference between dried and canned fruit as the children are tasting.

Other taste experiences for letter **A**: apples, avocado, and asparagus.

SONGS AND POEMS

Song: "I Am Learning Letter *A*"

(tune of "London Bridge")

I am learning letter **A**, letter **A**, letter **A**. I am learning letter **A**. Ă-ă-ă-ă. *(form capital A with fingers)*

A begins the alphabet, alphabet, alphabet. **A** begins the alphabet. Ă-ă-ă-ă. *(jump while singing)*

Apple starts with letter **A**, letter **A**, letter **A**. *Apple* starts with letter **A**. Ă-ă-ă-ă. *(make a round shape with hands)*

A B C D E F G H I J K L M N O P Q R S T U V W X Y Z!
(clap while singing)

Poem: "The Apple Tree"

Way up high in the apple tree, *(stretch hands overhead like a tree)*

Two little apples smiled down at me. *(fingers around eyes like glasses)*

I shook the tree as hard as I could. *(shaking motion)*

Down came the apples, *(bend down and touch the floor)*

MMMMMMMMMM, they were good! *(rub stomach)*

Poem: "Ant Hill"

Once I saw an ant hill *(hold hand in fist)*
With no ants about. *(Shake head)*
So, I called, "Little ants, *(look at fist)*
Won't you please come out?"
Then, as if they heard me call, *(cup hand to ear)*
One, two, three, four, five came out, *(hold up one finger at a time)*
And back they went again. *(close fist again)*

THE APPLE GAME

Teacher Directions: Cut out the apples and color the blank sides. Mark the other side of each wormless apple with a letter, word, number, or shape—whatever concept you would like your children to practice.

Student Directions: Spread out the apples, colored sides up. Take turns picking up an apple and telling what it says. If you do not know, put the apple back down. If you do know, you can keep the apple. If you get an apple with a worm, you must put it back. See how many apples you can get!

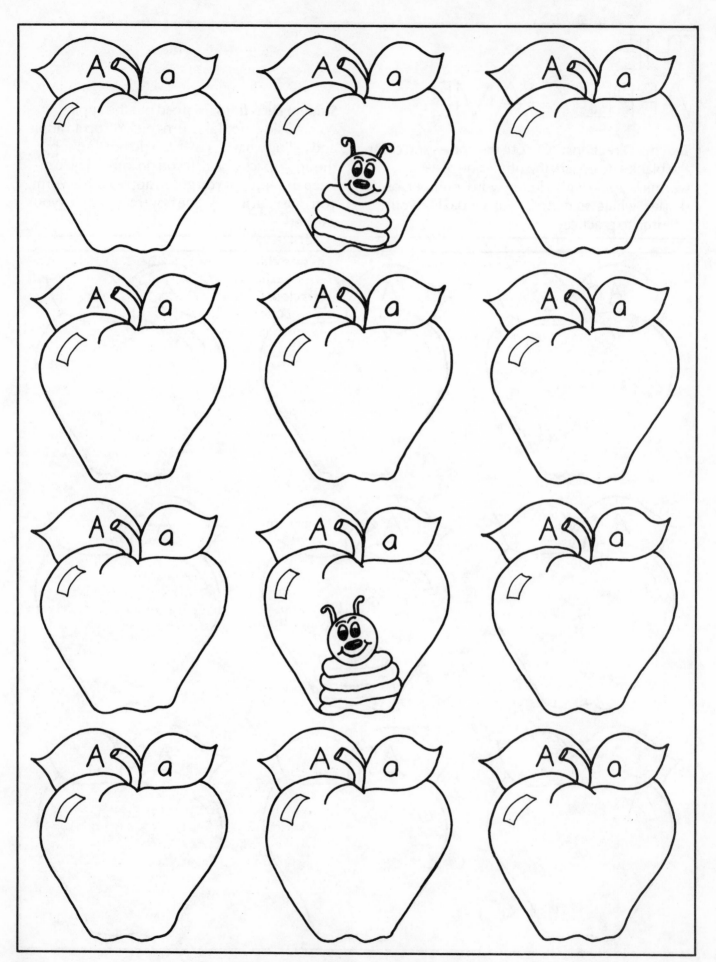

MOVEMENTS

Butterflies

Provide scraps of material or scarves for the children to hold. Play some gentle music and let the children pretend to be butterflies as they move around the play area waving the material. When you stop the music, the children must pretend to stop and rest on a flower. Repeat the activity, but this time have the butterflies fly around in pairs or triplets.

Boxes

Provide a jump rope or string for each child. Ask the children to form boxes with their ropes. Give directions for movements relative to the box, such as: "Jump into the box," "Jump out of the box," "Crawl around the box," "Hop on one foot around the box," "Keep jumping in and out of the box," "Crawl over the box on hands and feet." Let the children help think of other ways of moving in relation to the box. Ask the children to form a capital **B** with the rope, then a lower-case **b**.

Bean Bags

Provide a beanbag for each child or small group of children. Let them do the following movements with the beanbags:

- Walk with the beanbags on their heads or shoulders
- Throw them
- Play catch with them
- Throw them into a box or basket
- Kick them
- Walk like crabs, with the beanbags on their stomachs

Balloons

Give each child a balloon that is inflated and tied. Ask them to touch the balloon to the body part you call out. Use the terms *left* and *right* in your directions. Play music and let the children experiment with the balloons, moving them in many different ways. Encourage creativity. Tell them to bat their balloons and catch them. Tell the children to try not to let their balloons touch the floor. Have a contest to see who can keep their balloons in the air for the longest amount of time.

Bridges for *B*

Show the children how to form bridges with their bodies. Lie flat on your back on a mat. Place your hands close to your head with the palms of your hands on the mat. Push your body up using your arms and legs. Help the children who are not able to do this by holding them up. Have the children practice this exercise often to develop strength in their arms, stomachs, and legs.

Bucking Broncos

Teach the children to do this kicking exercise.
    First position: Stand up tall, with your hands on your hips.
    Second position: Squat down, putting your hands on the floor beside your feet.
    Third position: Kick your legs out behind you.
    Fourth position: Squat again. (Return to the first position.)
Have the children do this exercise slowly at first, while you count "one, two, three, four" at the various positions. Speed up the tempo as the children are able to accomplish this exercise.

GAMES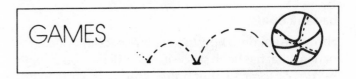

Basketball

Provide wastebaskets or boxes for the children to throw balls into. Let them keep score on paper or a chalkboard, tallying two points for every basket they make and counting their scores when play is finished. Graph the scores for a designated short period of time.

Bowling

Provide several balls and plastic bowling pins or plastic bottles to serve as bowling pins. The children can take turns rolling balls to knock over the pins. Have them call out the number of pins they knock down on each turn. Children can also take turns setting pins up again.

Busy Bees

Direct the children to find partners. The partners stand up facing each other. Call out a body part command such as "Nose to nose!" The children must perform that action. Call out as many different body parts as you can, using the terms *left* and *right* in your directions. Occasionally call out "Busy Bees!" The children must then run to find a new partner before the play continues.

Bouncing Balls

Provide balls for the children to practice bouncing. Tell the children to "pat" the ball—not to slap it. Let them bounce the balls back and forth with partners. Encourage the children to practice bouncing with both left and right hands.

Play this bouncing game after the children have had enough practice: Ask the children to form a circle. Give a ball to one of the children. That child walks around the circle bouncing the ball. Before returning to his or her place, the child calls out another child's name. The new player must get the ball and continue the game, bouncing the ball around the circle.

ALPHABET SNACK

Banana Boats

Show the children how to hollow a space in a peeled banana that has been set on its side. Fill the "boat" with berries or some peanut butter. Cut up the hollowed-out section into small bits and shape them into the letter **B**. If desired, sprinkle some wheat germ on the boat.

Other taste experiences for letter **B**: beans, beets, blueberries, bread, and Brussels sprouts.

SONGS AND POEMS

Song: *"B-B Bungle"*

(tune of "Hokey Pokey")

You put your back in, you take your back out.
You put your back in, and you bounce it all about.
You do the **B-B** Bungle and you bounce yourself about.
B-b-b-b-b-b *(make the sound of **B** while clapping)* B! *(say the name of the letter **B** and hold arms up above head)*

Other verses: Replace *back* with *body, bones, butterfly,* and *bunny.*
Actions: For *butterfly,* pretend to flap wings; for *bunny,* hop with hands forming ears on head.

Poem: "Busy Bumblebee"

A busy busy bumblebee buzzed by my bed.
Over me and under me, he landed on my head.
He buzzed by my ears and buzzed by my toes,
Then he sat down right on my nose!
(clap) Bye, busy bumblebee!

Actions: Hold thumb and index finger together to make a bee flying around to the places mentioned; wave goodbye as the bumblebee is scared away.

Poem: "Here Is a Bunny"

Here is a bunny *(make ears with fingers on head)*
With ears so funny.
And here is his hole in the ground. *(point to imaginary hole)*
If a noise he hears, *(clap loudly)*
He picks up his ears *(hold fingers up)*
Then runs to his home underground. *(run in place)*

BUSY BEE BINGO

Teacher Directions: Cut out the playing cards and the markers. Cut out the calling circles that you will use to keep track of what you call out.

Student Directions: Take a Busy Bee Bingo card. Count out nine markers for yourself. When the teacher calls out a letter or sound, mark your card. When you have a row going up and down, across, or on a diagonal, call out "Busy Bee Bingo!"

Markers:

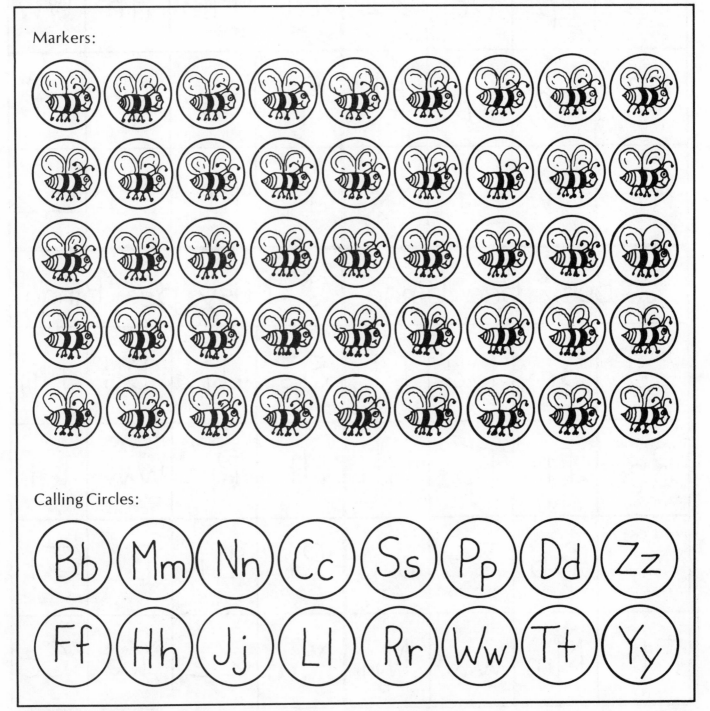

Calling Circles:

Bb Mm Nn Cc Ss Pp Dd Zz

Ff Hh Jj Ll Rr Ww Tt Yy

Busy Bee Bingo

Bb	Mm	Nn	Cc
Ss	Pp	Dd	Zz
Ff	Hh	Jj	Ll
Rr	Ww	Tt	Yy

Busy Bee Bingo

Bb	Jj	Tt	Cc
Ll	Mm	Hh	Ww
Pp	Ss	Nn	Ff
Yy	Ff	Dd	Zz

Busy Bee Bingo

Cc	Ss	Dd	Ll
Rr	Tt	Pp	Hh
Yy	Bb	Zz	Jj
Ff	Mm	Ww	Nn

Busy Bee Bingo

Ss	Jj	Dd	Nn
Hh	Pp	Ww	Ff
Rr	Ll	Bb	Tt
Mm	Zz	Yy	Cc

Cc

MOVEMENTS

Crawling Caterpillars

Provide a plastic tunnel through which the children may crawl. If you are not able to find one, make a tunnel out of tables, chairs, hula hoops, or tires. Ask the children to crawl forward and backward, in and out.

Cuddly Caterpillars

Divide the class into several groups. Ask them to lie on mats, on their backs, very close to each other. All heads should be at the same edge of the mat. Ask the first child to gently roll over the other caterpillars in the line. That child should stop at the end of the line and become still again as the second child rolls on down. Continue until everyone has had a turn to be a rolling, cuddly caterpillar.

Cobras

Show the children a picture of a cobra snake. Explain how it stretches and lifts up its head. Ask the children to pretend to be cobras. Tell them to lay on their stomachs on the floor. Keeping their legs on the floor and arms at their sides, they lift up the top part of their bodies, holding their heads up as high as they can.

Cleaning for Cobwebs

Ask the children to pretend to clean high corners for cobwebs. They can put on imaginary aprons and hold imaginary dust brooms. Tell them to jump up as high as possible, reaching and sweeping to remove the cobwebs. Let them work to some favorite music. When you stop the music, they can rest.

Cute Cats

Tell the children to pretend they are cats. Have them crawl around the playing area on hands and knees making cat sounds and movements. Tell them to take a cat nap when they hear you call "**C**!"

Candles

Ask the children to spread out over the playing area. Tell them to stand up very tall and pretend they are candles. Pretend to "light" them and let them slowly melt down to the floor.

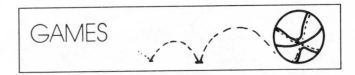

GAMES

Cat and Mice

Ask the children to form a circle. Choose four children to be "mice," and have them go into the center of the circle. Choose someone to be the cat, who must stand outside the circle. Call "Catch the mice!" The cat goes into the circle and tries to catch all the mice. (The mice cannot run outside the circle.) As the mice are tagged by the cat, they join the children in the circle. The last child to be caught becomes the next cat, and the play continues.

Corral Ball

Ask the children to form a circle. Provide about five or six balls for this game. The balls represent horses in the center of the circle, and the children represent the corral. Let the children roll the balls inside the circle. The children may use their hands or feet to keep the balls from rolling outside of the circle, but the children must remain in place. If a ball rolls outside the circle, they must leave it, as it is a "lost horse." Play the game until all the "horses" are lost.

Catch

Ask the children to stand in a circle. You stand in the center and throw the ball up into the air. Call a child's name. That child must come into the circle and catch the ball, then toss it back to you. Vary this game by tossing the ball to each child around the circle and having the child toss it back to you. Then bounce it to each child and have the child bounce it back. Use balloons or beanbags for tossing, instead of balls. Let the children play catch in pairs or in groups of three or four.

Coin Game

Provide several coins (or tokens to represent coins) and a jump rope or string for each child. Ask the children to form circles with their ropes. Tell them to stand back and throw coins into their circles. Have each child count the number of coins that land inside the circle. If the children play this game in pairs, they can help each other count.

ALPHABET SNACK

Crazy Cake

Divide the children into small groups. Let each small group make a "cake" of their own. Show the children how to cut the crusts from slices of whole wheat bread and roll them flat with a rolling pin. Let them spread one side of each slice of flattened bread with peanut butter. Stack the slices on top of each other. (Six to eight slices stack to a nice height.) "Frost" the cake with about ⅓ cup peanut butter. If your peanut butter is hard to spread, thin it with a tablespoon or two of fruit juice or milk. Provide cut-up carrots for the children to form the letter **C** on the top of their cakes. For fun, add a candle to each cake. Light them and sing "Happy **C** Week to You." Variation: Cream cheese can be substituted for the peanut butter for a different taste.

Other taste experiences for letter **C**: cabbage, coconut, carrots, cauliflower, celery, cheese, corn, cranberries, and cucumbers.

SONGS AND POEMS

Song: "C Is Coming Around the Corner"

(tune of "She'll Be Comin' Round the Mountain")

C is coming around the corner, C-c-c. *(hard sound of* **C***)*

(for **C***, make a* **C** *shape with hands; for* corner, *form hands into a square)*

C is coming around the corner, C-c-c. **C** is coming around the corner, **C** is coming around the corner, **C** is coming around the corner, C-c-c!

Other verses: Substitute *in a car, with a candle,* and *eating carrots* for *around the corner.*

Actions: For *in a car,* pretend to drive; for *with a candle,* hold up one finger; and for *eating carrots,* pretend to munch a carrot.

Poem: "Cute Curly Caterpillar"

Cute *(point with both hands to smiling face)*

Cute curly *(make curling motion with body)*

Cute curly caterpillar *(stand up straight with hands at sides, and wiggle body)*

Cute curly caterpillar crawling *(rub one hand up other arm)*

Cute curly caterpillar crawling, catching *(clap hands)*

Cute curly caterpillar crawling, catching crickets!
    (walk up one arm with two fingers of other hand)

CLOWN RECALL

Teacher Directions: Run off these pages on heavy paper. Cut apart and color in the clowns on the cards, making sure there is one exact duplicate of each clown.

Student Directions: Lay all the cards out on the playing area with the clowns facing down. Take turns turning over two cards. Try to match the clown pictures. If the cards don't match, turn them face down again. If you make a match, leave the cards face up and take another turn. If you turn over a **C** card, it will match with anything!

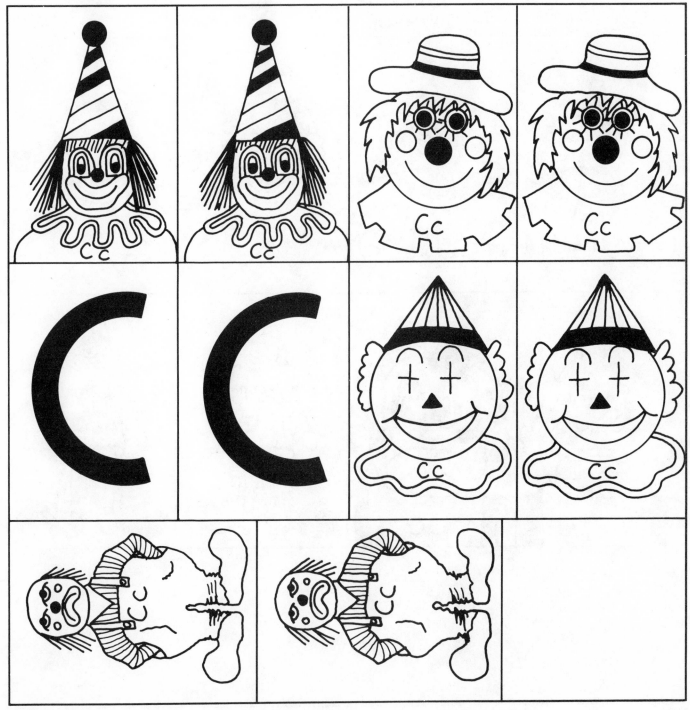

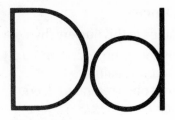

MOVEMENTS

Duckwalk

Show the children how to duckwalk—squatting down with hands on hips. Let the children waddle all around the play area in this fashion, greeting each other with quacks. Hold duckwalk races.

Dynamite

Ask the children to pretend to be sticks of dynamite. Ask them to crouch down as low as they can. When you clap your hands, they jump up as high as they can and "explode." Insist that they listen carefully and explode only when they hear a clap. Make some of the claps close together and space some out so the children have to wait and listen.

Diamonds

Provide each child with a jump rope or string, and ask them to form the shape of a diamond with it. Show them how to jump in and out of the diamond with their feet together. Ask them to jump over each of the four sides of their diamonds, coming back into the center each time. Let them change their diamond shapes into the letter **D**s.

Dancing

Play different kinds of music for the children. Let them dance the way the music makes them feel. Encourage creativity of movement. Try some mirror dancing. Let the children take turns being the image that everyone else imitates as the music plays. Divide the children into groups and let each group have the opportunity to "perform" for the others.

Donuts

Ask the children to try to form donut shapes with their bodies. Praise the ideas they invent. Ask them to make donuts in pairs and then make a class donut.

Dum-Ditty-Dum on a Drum

Tell the children to move about on the play area. Call out a movement, such as hopping, jumping in place, or bouncing a ball, and direct their movement by beating a drum. When the children hear the drum beat, they make the movement and repeat it as many times as you beat the drum. Call out a new movement to continue play.

GAMES

Drop the *D*

Ask the children to form a circle. Choose one child to be "It". "It" walks around the outside of the circle carrying a **D** (plastic letter), dropping it behind someone in the circle. That person picks up the **D** and chases "It" back to the empty spot in the circle. If "It" is tagged, the person who tagged him or her becomes "It." If "It" reaches the empty spot without being tagged, he or she remains "It." Play continues until everyone has had a turn.

Dodge Ball

Ask the children to form a circle facing inside. Choose three children to go inside the circle. Let the children on the outside of the circle roll balls into the circle and try to bump someone in the circle with a ball. The children inside the circle must try to dodge the ball. If a child is bumped by a ball, he or she exchanges places with the child who rolled the ball.

Dog Run

Ask the children to pretend to be dogs, bending over with hands and feet on the floor. Ask them to practice running in that position. Have the children race in relay teams. Each team might want to choose the name of a different kind of dog as its team name.

ALPHABET SNACK

Dunking Dip and a *D*

Let the children help measure out and mix together these ingredients:

1 cup sour cream
1 cup mayonnaise
1 tablespoon chopped onion
1 tablespoon dill weed

Spread the dip on plates or in pans for the children. Let the children "write" **D** in the dip with carrots, celery, and other firm vegetables before munching on them. If the children need a model for writing **D**, give each group a plastic letter or sheet of paper with **D** printed on it.

Other taste experiences for letter **D**: dill pickles, dates, dried fruit, and dumplings.

SONGS AND POEMS

Song: "This Old Dog"

(tune of "This Old Man")

This old dog, he played **D.**
He played **D** upon his drum.
With a **D**-d, **D**-d, **D**-d-d-d-d.
This dog played **D** on his drum. *(for "*d*," make the sound of* **D***; for* drum, *pretend to beat a drum; form a* **D** *with fingers when calling* **D***)*

Other verses: Substitute *desk, door, dirt,* and *dish* for *drum.*

Poem: "Duck Family"

Big white duck walked by, by, by. *(thumb up on right hand)*
Long-necked duck stretched high, high, high. *(forefinger up)*
Brave little duck went deep, deep, deep. *(middle finger down)*
Speckled little duck saw feet, feet, feet. *(ring finger down)*
Wee little duck said, "What can I do?" *(move small finger fast)*
Swim up the river to the little duck school. *(move all fingers fast)*

Poem: "Diddle Diddle Dance"

Teach the children a little dance to this nursery rhyme:

Diddle diddle dumpling; my son, John. *(clap hands, knees, thighs, and then hands again.)*
Went to bed with his stockings on. *(Pretend to sleep holding hands under head.)*
One shoe off and one shoe on. *(Hop on one foot, then on the other.)*
Diddle diddle dumpling; my son, John. *(Repeat the actions from the first line.)*

DAISY DOMINOES

Teacher Directions: Cut out and color in the dominoes.

Student Directions: Deal out four dominoes to each player. Put the rest of the dominoes in the center in a pile. Take turns placing dominoes down, matching the ends. If you cannot make a match, draw a domino from the pile. Try to match all dominoes.

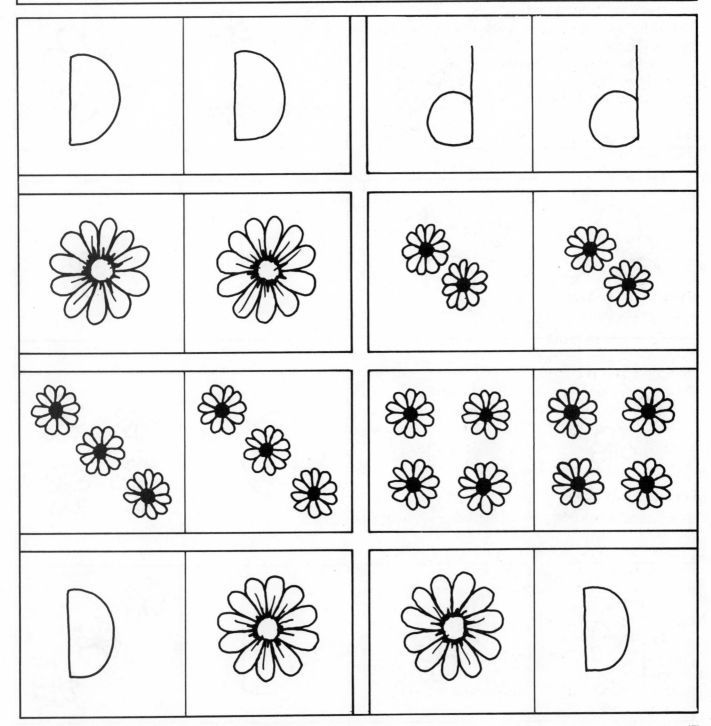

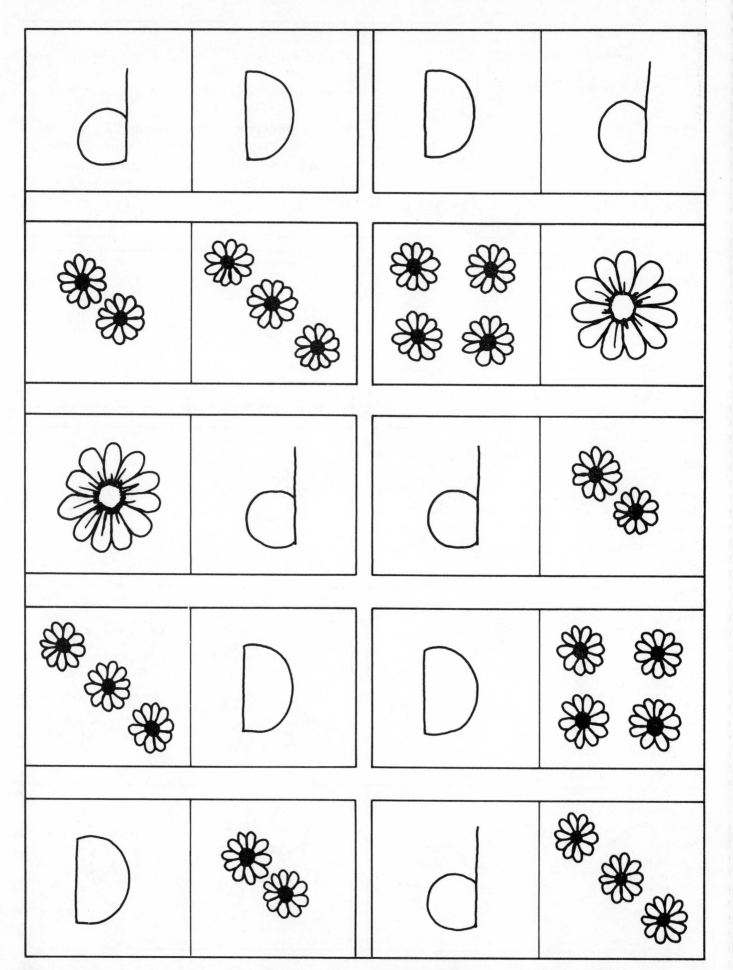

Ee

MOVEMENTS

Elephants

Show the children how to form an elephant trunk by holding their arms down in front of them and clasping their hands together. Ask them to pretend that they are very enormous elephants as they move about the play area swinging their trunks. Play some appropriate music for this movement.

Elephant Walk

Let the children go for an "elephant walk" in one long line. Ask everyone to stretch one hand each back through their legs and, with the other hand, take the outstretched hand of the person in front. The children will be lined up, attached like elephants holding trunks and tails. Have the "elephants" move to some slow music as they walk around.

Eels

Ask the children to lay down on the floor on their stomachs. Demonstrate how they should move by pulling themselves along using only their arms. Give them some directions for moving such as: move forward, move backward, roll over to the left, roll over to the right, curl up, move fast, and move slow.

Eel Rope Exercises

Provide each child with a jump rope or length of string. Ask them to lay it out in a line and pretend that it is an eel. Tell them to make these motions: run, walk, gallop, hop, and skip around it; walk and hop backward around it; jump over it forward and backward; walk heel to toe around it; jump rope with it.

Echo an Exercise

Talk with the children about what an echo is. Have them echo some things you call out. Then have them try to echo (imitate) exercises that you begin. Tell them to be very quiet and do with their bodies only what you show them, such as toe-touching or jumping jacks. They must repeat each exercise as many times as you do it. Use exercises you have taught the children—ones they have accomplished successfully.

Eggs

Let the children pretend to be animals (chick, duck, snake, turtle) that hatch from eggs. Together, the children should act out the movements of trying to break out of the shell. Play some joyous music when everyone is out of the egg. Let everyone move around the way the animals they chose would move.

Egg Roll

Bring an egg to school and let everyone gently feel it. Talk about its shape. Lay it down and roll it around so the children can see the action. Ask the children to try to form their bodies into egg shapes. Tell them to grasp their knees to keep themselves rolled up tightly. Let them roll around on mats, rolling from side to side.

Elevators

Let the children pretend to be elevators going up and down. Perform the action with them. Go up and down very slowly and then speed up. This exercise will help strengthen the children's leg muscles. Try this variation: Ask the children to sit on the floor with their feet extended in front of them. With their hands on the floor at their sides, they try to lift their bodies up as much as they can.

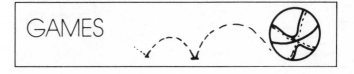

GAMES

Egg Carton Toss

Give each child an empty egg carton. Ask them to put the cartons on the floor and move a few steps back from them. Ask them to toss, one at a time, a handful of beans or other small objects into the egg cartons. When they are finished, each child should count how many objects landed in the sections of the egg carton.

19

Elephant Soccer

Ask the children to form a circle, each child standing with feet wide apart. Ask them to hold their arms down in front of them with their hands clasped for trunks. Let them roll a ball across the circle trying to get it through someone's legs. The children may use only their trunks to stop the ball. If the ball does go out of the circle through someone's legs, that person must run and get it and bring it back. Add more balls to the circle as the children become proficient.

ALPHABET SNACK

Elephant Ears

6 eggs
2 cups milk
3 tablespoons shortening, melted
1½ cups whole wheat flour
1 teaspoon salt
3 teaspoons sugar

Break the eggs into a big bowl. Let children help beat them. Measure and add milk and shortening, then beat again. Add flour, salt, and sugar, and mix well. Heat some oil in an electric skillet. Pour the batter in four- or five-inch circles. Cook until browned, then flip and brown the other side. Let the children spread their Elephant Ears with butter or applesauce. Ask them to form the letter **E** with raisins on top of their Elephant Ears before they roll up and eat the snack.

Other taste experiences for letter **E**: eggs, eggplant, and English muffins.

SONGS AND POEMS

Song: "I've Got the Letter *E*"

(tune of "He's Got the Whole World in His Hands")

I've got the letter **E** for elephant. *(make trunk like an elephant)*
I've got the letter **E** for elephant.
I've got the letter **E** for elephant.
E for elephant.
I've got the letter **E** for egg. *(form hands into oval shape)*

I've got the letter **E** for egg.
I've got the letter **E** for egg.
E for egg.
I've got the letter **E** for echo, echo. *(cup hands around mouth repeating the word* echo)
I've got the letter **E** for echo, echo.
I've got the letter **E** for echo, echo.
E for echo, echo.
E makes this sound: ĕ-ĕ-ĕ. *(stamp feet on the sound of short* **E**)
E makes this sound: ĕ-ĕ-ĕ.
E makes this sound: ĕ-ĕ-ĕ.
E goes ĕ-ĕ-ĕ.

Poem: "The Elephant"

He's ever so big and ever so fat. *(hold hands high and then apart)*
He has no hands, he has no toes. *(shake finger and head for* no)
But goodness gracious, *(hands on cheeks)*
Such a nose! *(put right fist on nose and go down, making an imaginary trunk)*

Poem: "Circus Elephant"

I am a circus elephant. *(point to self)*
See the trunk on me? *(make a trunk with arms)*
I'm very big and very fat, *(lift hands high and then apart sideways for fat)*
And on my head I wear a hat. *(point to head and make a hat with hands above head)*

EGGHEAD PUZZLE

Teacher Directions: Duplicate one "egghead" for each player. Color each egghead a different color. Cut apart each egghead and put it into an envelope labeled with its color word. Cut out and tape the gameboard to the floor. Provide a beanbag or cube to toss.

Student Directions: Choose a color for your "egghead." Take turns throwing the beanbag or cube. It if falls on the **E** section, find that part of your egghead. If it falls on **e**, build that onto your egghead. If it lands on a part you already have put together, let the next player have a turn. See who can finish building their eggheads!

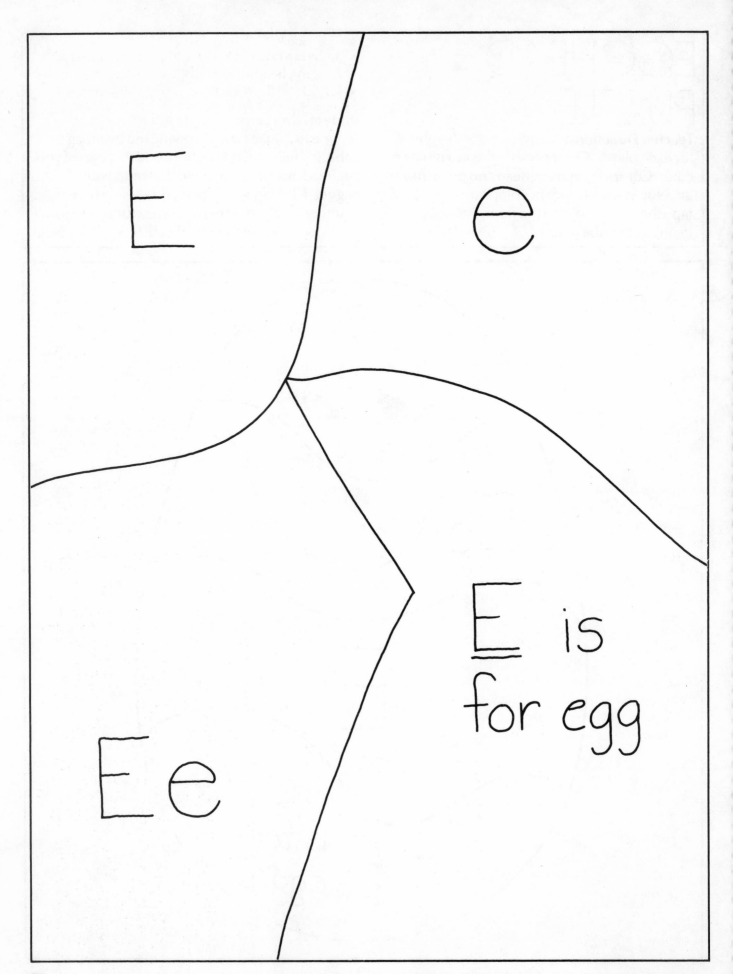

E

e

E is
for egg

Ee

Ff

MOVEMENTS

Frogs

Show the children how to do a frog leap. Begin from a crouched position. Let them practice making short leaps, long leaps, fast leaps, and slow leaps. Play some music and let the children leap around, pretending to be in a large swamp. Lay out mats as lily pads so that the frogs can land on them to rest.

Fireflies

Tell the children to pretend to be fireflies. Explain that when you play music, they can move all around the play area. When the music stops, they must freeze. Ask all the fireflies to lie on the floor in the shape of letter **F** when they are finished.

Feathers

Provide a small feather for each child. Ask the children to stand on the play area without touching anyone else. Let them experiment with different things to do with their feathers. Let them try throwing it, catching it, moving around it, blowing it, dancing with it, letting it fly, and so on. Have small groups of children write **F** and **f** in the air with their feathers. Call out commands for the children to perform with the feathers such as: "Hold it high with your right hand," "Wave it with your left hand," and "Set it on your right foot."

Floor Work

Ask the children to do several exercises lying on the floor. Have them try sit-ups, push-ups, bicycles, and angels in the snow. Ask the children to lie on their stomachs, roll over quickly, and get up into the sitting position. Have them roll from both the right and left sides. Ask them to roll from their backs up into the sitting position also.

Flip-Flops

Show the children how to do this exercise. With hands on waist, bend forward (from the waist), then to the left side, to the back, then to the right side. Bend in each direction to the count of eight. Repeat that progression with four counts, then two, then one, and finally stretching all around several times.

GAMES

Frog in the Sea

Ask the children to stand in a circle facing in. Choose one child to be the frog that stands in the center of the circle. Teach everyone this chant: "Frog in the sea, can't catch me." Tell the children to quickly squat down on the word *me*. The frog tries to catch someone by tapping the person on the head before he or she is in the squatting position. The person tagged becomes the new frog, and the game continues.

Follow the Leader

Give each child a jump rope. Let the children take turns standing in front of the group performing some movement with the rope. The rest of the children must copy that movement. Give the children the opportunity to practice jumping rope when this game is finished.

Four and Five

Divide your class into groups of four or five. Let each group think of an **F** creature (such as fish, frog, or fox) to act out. Tell the other children to guess what it is. When it is guessed, let all the children act it out.

Farmer in the Dell

Play this game the traditional way and then repeat it using **F** things such as "The farmer takes a fan . . .," and so forth. Let the children think of the things to be used in the song before each verse. Each time you play, encourage the children to think of items they have not sung before.

Fast Time

Talk about the word *fast* and what it means. Tell the children to perform these movements: walk fast, run fast, tiptoe fast, skip fast, jump fast, hop fast, heel-to-toe walk fast, and crawl fast. Then ask them to repeat the movements, but this time *not* fast. Ask them which they liked better. Test everyone's "fastness" by holding races. Ask everyone to call out "**F**" when they finish a race.

ALPHABET SNACK

Fondue for *F*

½ cup cheddar cheese
½ cup Swiss cheese
2 tablespoons oil
2 tablespoons flour
1 ½ cup milk

Let each child have a turn to grate a little of the cheeses. In a pan, heat the oil. Stir in the flour. Slowly stir in the milk and cook until slightly thickened. Add grated cheeses and stir constantly until melted. Give each child a piece of French bread cut into squares for dipping. Ask them to lay out their bread squares in the shape of the letter **F**. Pour the warm cheese into several bowls so the children can eat in small groups. Show them how to put their bread cubes on a plastic fork to swirl in the cheese.

Other taste experiences for letter **F**: French fries, figs, fish, frankfurters, French toast, fritters, and fruits.

SONGS AND POEMS

Song: "The Farmer in the Field"

(tune of "The Farmer in the Dell")

The farmer in the field, the farmer in the field,
F-f-f-f-f-f *(sound of* **F***)*, the farmer in the field.

The farmer takes a friend . . .

Other verses: Continue as in "The Farmer in the Dell," using *frog, fox, fish,* **F**, and finally:

The **F** stands alone, the **F** stands alone,
F-f-f-f-f-f, the **F** stands alone. *(stand and clap hands above head)*

Poem: "Funny Funny Froggie"

Funny funny froggie, hop hop hop.
Funny funny froggie, stop stop stop.
Funny funny froggie, run and play.
Funny funny froggie, don't run away!

Recite this poem miming the actions three times—the first time to a regular tempo, the second time fast, and the third time very slow.

FENCE
THE FROG

Teacher Directions: Duplicate one frog game-board for each player. Cut out the markers. There should be 11 markers per player. Use flashcards for numbers, letters, sounds, or words.

Student Directions: Take a frog sheet and some markers. Take turns drawing a flashcard to answer. If you are right, place a marker to build your fence. See if you can put a fence around your frog!

F f	F f	F f	F f	F f	F f	F f	F f
F f	F f	F f	F f	F f	F f	F f	F f
F f	F f	F f	F f	F f	F f	F f	F f
F f	F f	F f	F f	F f	F f	F f	F f
F f	F f	F f	F f	F f	F f	F f	F f

MOVEMENTS

Grasshoppers

Ask the children to pretend they are grasshoppers in the green grass. Let them jump around with big leaps. Tell them to make the sound of the letter **G** as they land. Call out "Grasshoppers, go!" and "Grasshoppers, stop!" to make more of a game out of this activity.

Grapes in a Bunch

Ask all the children to stand together in a "bunch." Pretend to "pluck" one child at a time away from the bunch by tapping the child on the shoulder. Tell the children to roll away on the floor as they are removed from the bunch. Point a direction for each grape to roll.

Ghosts

Ask the children to pretend to be spooky ghosts. Play some appropriate ghost music to accompany movement. Tell them they must be very silent ghosts and do their frightening without making noises with their voices. Encourage them to be imaginative in their movements.

Garbage Can Fun

Bring a large clean green garbage can. Let the children crawl into and out of it, sit in it, or use it to play games. One game to play is "Ghost Noises." Ask the children to stand in a circle. Place the green garbage can in the center. Blindfold one child and choose another to get in the garbage can. Tell the child in the garbage can to call out, "Green ghosts like green garbage cans, G-g-g-g (hard sound of **G**)." The blindfolded child must guess who is in the garbage can. If you are unable to get a garbage can, adapt the game using a green blanket or sheet.

Gorilla Walk

Show the children how to do the gorilla walk. Grasp your ankles with your hands and move around. Have a gorilla race and pretend to run for bananas.

Get Up, Go Down

Assign the children partners for this sit-ups exercise. Ask one to hold the feet of the other. Then have the partners trade positions.

Go for *G*

Give each child a jump rope. Ask them to lay the ropes on the floor in the shape of letter **G**. Tell them to gallop around their own **G**s and those of the other children. When they have had time to circle a lot of **G**s, ask them each to return to his or her own rope. Ask them to pick up the ropes and jump each time you say "Go." Call it out slowly and only one at a time in the beginning. Then, say "Go, go" for the children to jump twice, then more rapidly if they are able.

GAMES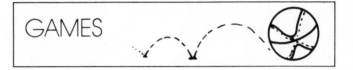

Galloping Ghosts

Divide the class into groups of six or seven. Ask the groups to form circles. Choose one person to be the galloping ghost. Instruct the children to pass a ball to one another in the circle. The galloping ghost runs around outside the circle trying to tag whomever has the ball. If the ghost is successful, the tagged person becomes the new ghost. Play until everyone has had a chance to be the galloping ghost.

Go, Geese, Go

Tell the children to stand in a column with their hands on the waist of the person in front. Choose one child to be the ghost. The children in the column are the geese. To begin the game, the ghost stands in front of the column, facing the first child. At the signal **G**, the ghost runs to the end of the line of geese, trying to tag the last goose. The line of geese tries to maneuver around to protect the last goose from being caught. If the ghost is successful, choose someone else to be the ghost. Divide the class into groups of 6–8 to play this game.

ALPHABET SNACK

Ghosts and Goblins

Show the children how to spread cottage cheese or vanilla yogurt on a plate in the shape of a ghost. Let them finish the ghost by placing halved grapes as eyes. Ask them to form the letter **G** with some granola on the body of the ghost.

Other taste experiences for letter **G**: grapefruit, grapes, grated cheese, green beans, and green peppers.

SONGS AND POEMS

Song: "Three Good Ghosts"

(tune of "Three Blind Mice")

Three good ghosts. Three good ghosts.
See how they go. See how they go. *(for go, pump arms back and forth as in running)*
They go, go, go for the letter **G**. G-g-g-g-g-g-g-g! *(hard sound of **G**)*
Did you ever see such ghosts in your life, for **G**, **G**, **G**! *(letter name)*

Other verses: Substitute *golf* and *gallop* for *go*.
Actions: For *golf*, pretend to hit a ball with a club; for *gallop*, gallop around while singing.

Poem: "Grandma's Glasses"

These are Grandma's glasses. *(make rings around eyes with fingers)*
This is Grandma's cap. *(with hands, make a pointed hat on head)*
These are Grandma's hands. *(hold up hands)*
Folded in her lap. *(fold hands gently in lap)*

Poem: "Ghosts"

Great big ghost on a great big hill.
Teeny tiny ghost on a teeny tiny hill. *(stretch hands up and down for big and tiny)*
Great big, teeny tiny, great big, teeny tiny.
Now I'm a person standing still.

Poem: "Ghost in the Garden"

A ghost goes in our garden, our garden, our garden.
A ghost goes in our garden, and eats up everything green.
He gulps **G** and he gulps **G** and he gulps **G** and he gulps **G**. *(hard **G** sound)*
A ghost goes in our garden and gulps up everything green.

GO, GHOST, GO!

Teacher Directions: Cut apart the letter flash-cards. Duplicate a ghost for each player. Cut apart the ghosts and put the pieces in envelopes.

Student Directions: Put your ghost together. Watch as the teacher shows you a letter. Each time it is your turn and you can say a word beginning with the letter, make one part of your ghost disappear. Can you make your whole ghost disappear? You can try to make your ghost appear again, too, by playing the game backwards.

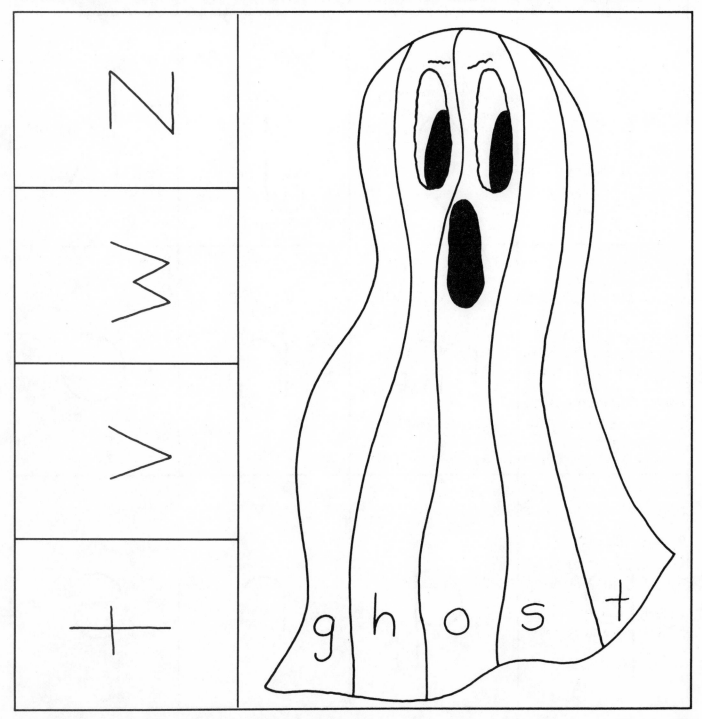

b	c	d	f
g	h	j	k
l	m	n	o
p	q	r	s

Alphabet Fun and Games reproducible page, copyright © 1984 Pitman Learning, Inc.

Hh

MOVEMENTS

Hula Hoops

Provide some hula hoops for the children to work with individually or in small groups. Let them: roll and catch them; run through them; jump rope with them; roll them to each other; lay them on the floor to hop in and out of; swing them around hips, neck, arms, or legs; and throw balls through them. Play "Hula Hoop Hunt": Lay the hula hoops out on the floor or playground. Instruct the children to run around. When you blow your whistle, tell them to come and each sit down inside a hula hoop.

Hands

Talk about all the things our hands help us to do. Distribute balls to the children. Let them work in pairs to perform these movements with the balls: roll, bounce, catch and throw, toss up high, dribble, and throw into a basket or box. After spending some time with these activities, the children can play with the balls without using their hands. See what they discover from this experience!

Horses

Let the children pretend to move as horses. Ask them to fold their arms on their chests and gently throw their heads upward and back, "tossing their manes." As they prance about the play area, they can point their toes. Play some lively music to accompany the movement. Ask them if they can feel all the muscles they are using as they do this exercise.

Humpty Dumpty

Ask the children to stand up very tall. Tell them to jump down to a crouch each time you call **H**, as if they were falling off a wall. Call all the letters of the alphabet in mixed order as you play this game. To end the game, let the children recite the alphabet with you. When you get to **H**, everyone should fall down on the floor. Ask the children to lie flat on the floor until you call their names softly.

Hopping

Talk with the children about different animals (rabbits, kangaroos, and frogs) that hop to move around. Let them pretend to be those animals. Teach the children the bunny hop. Divide the children into teams and have hopping races.

Hawks

Show the children a picture of a hawk. Talk about how this bird moves. Explain how it swoops down to pick up things. Give each child a cut-out **H** for this exercise as they pretend to be hawks. Tell them to drop the **H**, then swoop down to pick it up. Let them exchange **H**'s with their friends, swooping to exchange them.

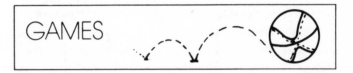
GAMES

Hens and Chickens

This is an excellent game for a rainy day when the children must play indoors. Choose one child to be the hen. That child leaves the room. The other children sit in a circle. Choose one child to be the baby chick. Ask the hen to return to the circle with closed eyes and to say "Cluck, cluck." The chosen child answers, "Peep, peep." The hen, with open eyes, then points to whomever he or she thinks made the sound. If the hen is right, the baby chick becomes the hen, and the game continues. This game can also be played a different way: A hen is chosen and leaves the room. Pick five children to be baby chicks. All the children in the room sit at desks or tables with their heads down and faces covered. Ask the hen to return to find her baby chicks by listening for the peeps coming from the children you chose. When the hen has found the five chicks, choose new chicks and a new hen and continue the game.

Hunting and Finding

Make about 40 hats from colored construction paper. Divide the class into two groups. Let each group choose a name for themselves such as horses or hippos. Tell one group to cover their eyes while the other group hides the hats. Explain that the hats must be hidden so that part of each one shows just a little. They must not be completely covered. When they are all hidden, tell the other group to find them. Count to see that 40 were found. Reverse roles of the groups. To reinforce the sound of the letter **H**, tell the children to call out the letter each time they find a hat.

Happy Hippo

Ask the children to stand on a line that is marked on the play area. Show them another line that they will run to, approximately 60 feet away from them. Choose one child to be "It." "It" stands midway between the two lines. When you call "Happy Hippo," the children run to the opposite goal line, trying not to be tagged by "It." Those who are tagged remain in the center and try to catch other children as the game continues. The last child to be tagged will be "It" for the next game.

Halt

Ask the children to find a place on the play area where they have plenty of room for movement. Call out movements for them to make. When you blow your whistle and call "Halt," they must freeze and listen for the next movement you call. Use movements such as hopping, jumping, running, skipping, crawling, leaping, slithering, sliding, galloping, and moving backward.

ALPHABET SNACK

Humpty With a Hat

For each child you will need:

    1 hard-boiled egg
    1 thick tomato slice
    Other vegetables cut up in small pieces

Cut a hole in the middle of each tomato slice big enough for the egg to "sit" in. The cut-out tomato section becomes a hat for the "Humpty" egg. Let them make faces on Humpty by sticking vegetable pieces into the egg with toothpicks. Have the children use other cut-up vegetable pieces to form the letter **H** on the plate for Humpty to look at.

Other taste experiences for letter **H**: hamburger, honey, and honeydew melons.

SONGS AND POEMS

Song: "Ha-Ha Hippo"

(tune of "Baa Baa Black Sheep")

Ha-ha Hippo, have you any hair? *(point to hair)*
Hurrah, hurrah, you have hair. *(for hurrah, shake arms in air as if cheering)*
Hair for my horse and hair for my hog,
And hair for my **H**, ha-ha-ha-ha-ha!
Ha-ha Hippo, have you any hair?
Hurray, hurray, you have hair.

Other verses: Substitute *hats, hammers,* and *houses* for *hair.*

Actions: For *hats,* put hands over head; for *hammers,* pretend to pound; for *houses,* make imaginary roof over head.

Poem: "Happy's Hammers"

(Have the children sit on the floor with their legs out in front of them.)

Happy works with one hammer, one hammer, one hammer. *(pound one hand on floor)*
Happy works with one hammer, then he works with two.
Happy works with two hammers, two hammers, two hammers. *(pound with both hands)*
Happy works with two hammers, then he works with three.
Happy works with three hammers, three hammers, three hammers. *(pound with both hands and one leg)*
Happy works with three hammers, then he works with four.
Happy works with four hammers, four hammers, four hammers. *(pound with both hands and both legs)*
Happy works with four hammers, then he works with five.
Happy works with five hammers, five hammers, five hammers. *(pound with both hands and both legs and move head)*
Happy works with five hammers, then he goes to sleep. *(lean forward and lay head down on hands)*

HI HO HIPPO

Teacher Directions: Duplicate a hippo and a set of hats for each player. Color each hippo a different color. Cut out and color the hats. Attach a spinner by inserting a brass fastener through a large paper clip and into the center of the circle with the color words. Color in these sections.

Student Directions: Choose a hippo. Pick eight hats, one of each color—red, yellow, orange, blue, green, purple, black, and brown. Take turns spinning the spinner. Put the colored hat on your hippo. Try to get all eight hats on your hippo. If you spin a color you already have, it is the next player's turn.

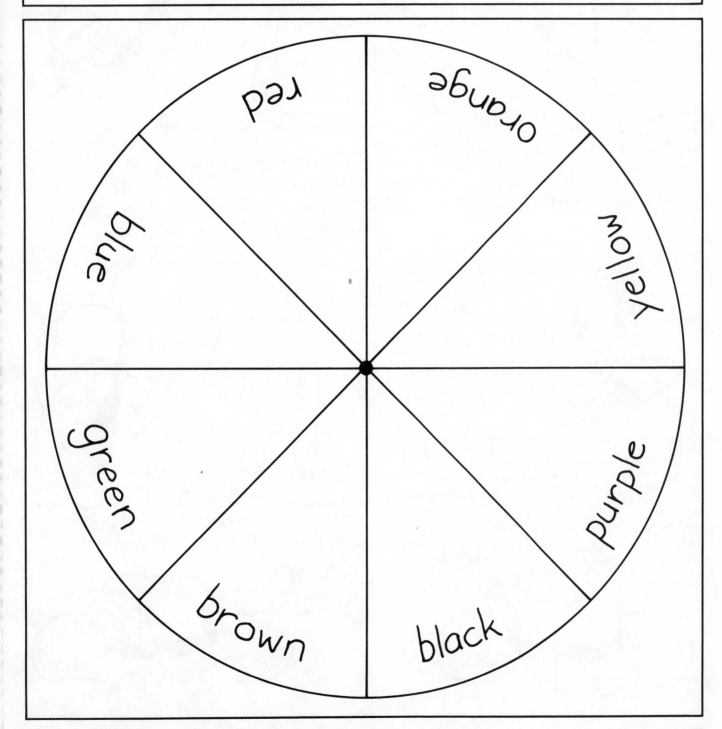

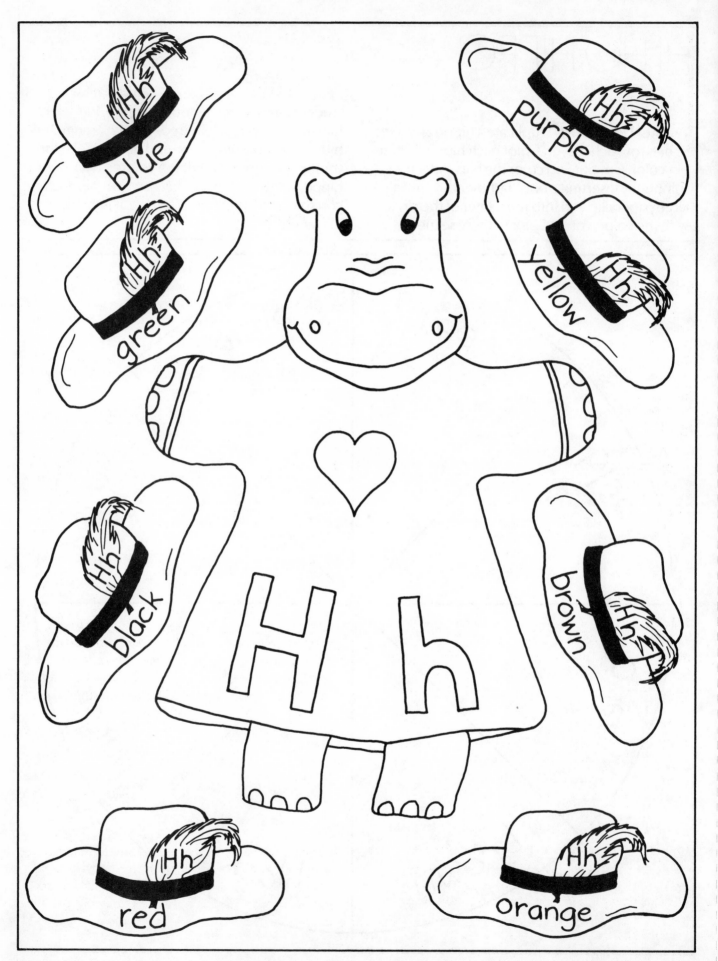

blue

purple

green

yellow

black

brown

H h

red

orange

Ii

Insects

Ask the children to pretend to move as insects. Let them crawl on their hands and knees or their hands and feet around the play area. Ask them to tell what insects they are imitating. Play some creepy crawly music for them to move to. Ask them to greet other insects by saying "I."

Iguanas

Show the children a picture of an iguana and provide some information about it. Let them pretend to move about the play area as iguanas. Ask them to crawl around holding their bodies as low to the floor as possible, propelling themselves with bent arms and legs. When you call out I, ask them to stop and move their heads slowly from side to side and make the sound of letter I.

I Tightrope

Tape or chalk a large capital I on the play area. Ask the children to pretend to be tightrope walkers. Show them how to walk heel-to-toe along the lines of the letter. Ask them to try walking sideways and backward along the I.

Instruments

Teach the children to use a variety of rhythm instruments. Let them play along as you all sing favorite songs. Have a rhythm parade, singing and playing instruments and marching around. If instruments are inaccessible, improvise. Fill coffee cans with marbles to shake. Beat on cans with tinker toy sticks. Bang spoons on pans and lids. Staple together aluminum foil pie pans with a few toothpicks inside to shake. Bang blocks together to the beat. Let the children help by contributing ideas for making other things around them into rhythm instruments.

Indian Drum

Explain to the children that American Indians used drums to send messages to one another. Tell them that they will do the same thing now. Show them a movement to make. Whenever they hear the drum, they must move as many times as the drum is beaten. If the drum beats with a fast continuous beat, they must move quickly until the drumming stops. When the drum is quiet, instruct them to freeze. Direct movements such as walking, tiptoeing, skipping, hopping, crawling, leaping, and galloping.

Imagination

Talk with the children about using their imaginations. Let them pretend to be some of the following things: a very fat person on a crowded bus, a tiny grain of salt falling from a shaker, jello or pudding, a motorcycle rider, a firecracker exploding, a ball being bounced, a hamburger frying, an icicle melting, or a toy car. Give the children the opportunity to help think of other things they might try to act out.

Inch-Foot

This game is similar to red light/green light. Choose one player to be the caller. This person should stand on a line marked with tape or chalk. Have the other children stand in a row opposite the caller, about 30 feet away. Facing the group, the caller calls "Inch," and the row of children take tiny steps toward the marked line. At irregular intervals, the caller turns with back toward the group and calls "Foot." The children then take heel-to-toe steps. The game continues with alternate "Inch" and "Foot" calls until one of the children reaches the marked line. That child becomes the new caller.

I-I Over

Ask the children to sit in a circle facing in. Place a stack of blocks representing the letter I in the center of the circle. Let the children roll a ball at the I, trying to knock it over. The child who is successful at knocking it over must quickly set the I back up, and the game continues. Divide your class into smaller groups to play this game to give the children more opportunities to play.

The Island Game

Set out as many carpet squares on the play area as there are children. (If you do not have carpet squares, pieces of material or paper will suffice.) Tell the children that these represent islands in the sea. Ask the children to pretend to swim around in the sea while they hear music. When the music stops, they must swim to an island immediately. Only one child at a time can "inhabit" an island. Each time you begin the music again, remove one island. If children do not get an island, they must come and sit by you, pretending they have been rescued by a ship. Play until there is only one island left.

Poem: "The Inchworms Are Creeping"

The inchworms are creeping, shhh shhh shhh!
The inchworms are creeping, shhh shhh shhh!
They do not make a sound as their feet touch the ground.
The inchworms are creeping, shhh shhh shhh!
(on creeping, *move fingers along forearm; on* shhh, *raise fingers to lips)*

ALPHABET SNACK

Igloos

Serve each child a halved peach or pear (rounded side up) on a plate. Show the children a picture of an Eskimo igloo. Then give them some vanilla yogurt to cover their fruit halves, making them look like frozen igloos. Let them form the letter **I** on the igloo with raisins, nuts, or seeds. Variation: Use cottage cheese or whipped cream to cover the fruit.

Other taste experiences for letter **I**: Irish soda bread and homemade ice cream.

SONGS AND POEMS

Song: "Itsy Itsy Inchworm"

(tune of "Eentsy Weentsy Spider")

The itsy itsy inchworm inched up the letter **I**. *(make fingers of one hand crawl up the opposite arm)*
Down came the ink and washed the inchworm out. *(move hands in a downward motion)*
Out came the sun and dried up all the ink, *(make a large round shape with arms to represent the sun)*
So the itsy itsy inchworn inched up the **I** again. *(make fingers of one hand crawl up the opposite arm)*

INCHWORM COUNTING PUZZLE

Teacher Directions: Duplicate the pages so you have one inchworm for each child. Color each inchworm a different color. Cut apart the inchworms and put the pieces in envelopes.

Student Directions: Take an envelope. Put together the inchworm by putting the numbers in order.

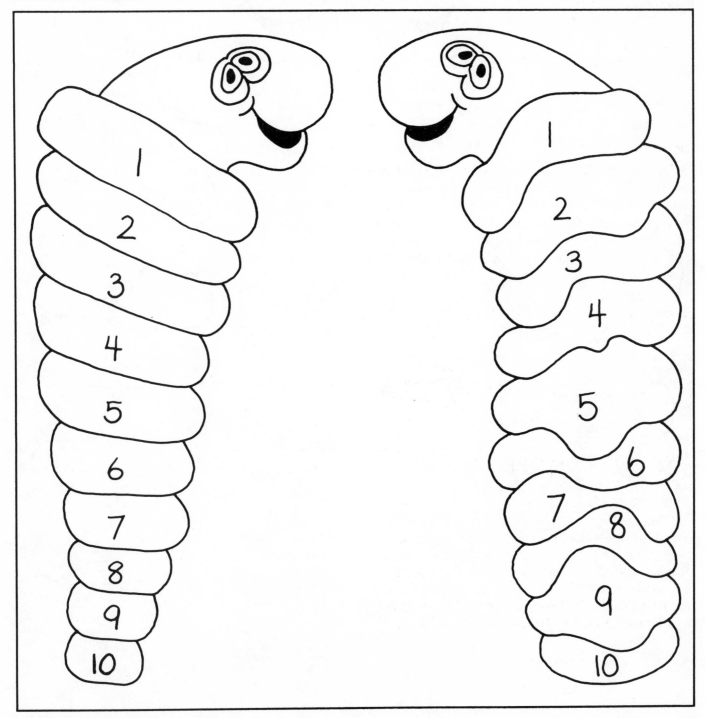

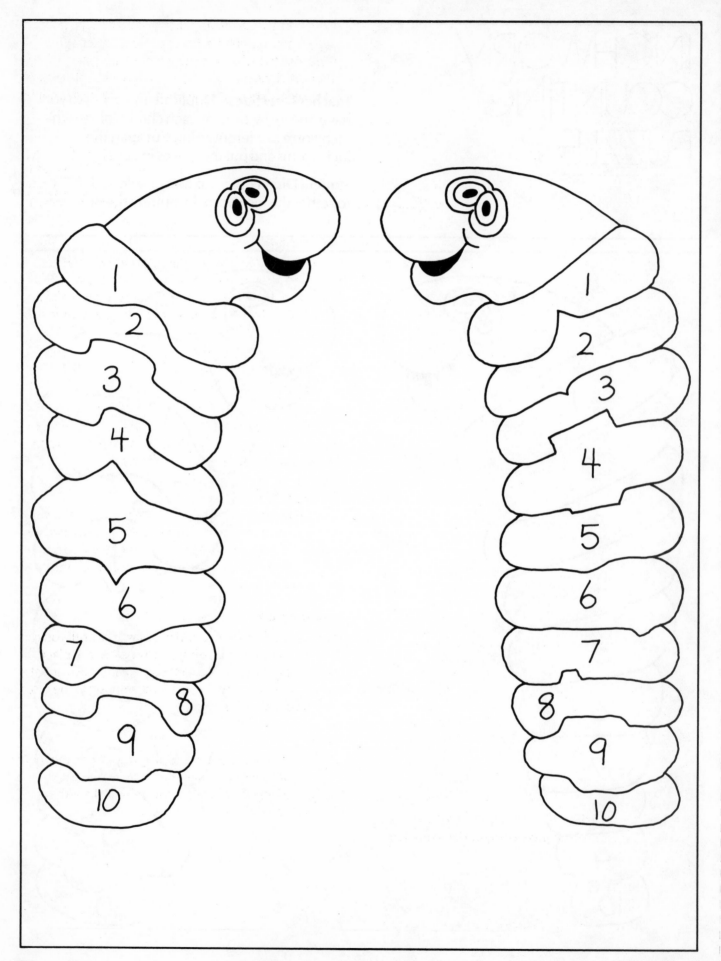

Alphabet Fun and Games reproducible page, copyright © 1984 Pitman Learning, Inc.

Jj

MOVEMENTS

Jungle Creatures

Ask the children to name creatures that live in the jungle. Let the children move like those creatures they name. If the children have a difficult time thinking of animals, read a jungle picture story before you begin this activity.

Jumping Balls

Provide each child with a ball. Assign a windowless area for the children to play. A gymnasium or outdoor handball court or tennis backboard would be ideal. Ask them to throw the balls up high on the wall to see how high they can make the balls "jump." Tell them to try to catch the balls when they come back down. Show the children how to throw both underhand and overhand.

Jump Through Hands

Teach this exercise to your children: Ask them to squat on the floor with their arms forward and their hands on the floor. Keeping their hips bent and their knees tucked up, they jump, bringing their legs through their arms. See if they can reverse the direction of the jump!

Jazzexercise

Play some different pieces of jazz music for the children to listen to. Ask them how the music makes them feel. Tell them to move around the way the music makes them feel. Direct some exercises to jazz music. Or create simple routines for the children to learn, if they are interested in choreographed steps. Let the children each have a chance to volunteer to lead the exercises.

Jump Rope Jamboree

Provide a jump rope for each child. Ask the children to lay their ropes out in the shape of the letter J. Tell them to perform these movements around their Js: jump, jigglewalk, jog, and jet. Let them practice jumping rope. Ask them to try jogging while they jump if they are proficient enough. If the children are able to jump to a jingle, they might use the first "j" poem as a jingle.

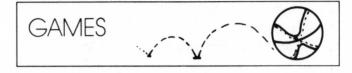

GAMES

Jack-a-Dandy

Ask the children to form a large circle. Make a set of large, cardboard lollipops, one of each color, and lay them in the center of the circle. Choose one child to be blindfolded and another to pick up and hide a lollipop; the rest of the children will chant:

> Little Jack-a-Dandy
> Had a stick of candy.
> Everytime he took a bite
> A piece went quickly out of sight.

The blindfolded child identifies the color of the missing lollipop. Play until all children have had a turn to be blindfolded and to hide a lollipop.

Jump Over the J

Cut a J from paper and lay it on the floor. Ask the children to form a line and take turns jumping over it, trying not to touch it. Give everyone more chances to play by making several Js and dividing the children into small groups.

Jog and Jump

Let the children jog around the play area until you call "Jump." They stop jogging and jump once in place, then stand still until you call "Jog" again. Add a greater sense of direction to the game by pointing in the direction you want them to jog.

Jacks

Work with the children in small groups, showing them how to play jacks. Let them begin by working with only one jack and a ball, adding more jacks as they become proficient.

ALPHABET SNACK

Jungle Joy

Provide for each child:

½ cup milk
1 small banana or a half of a larger one
1 tablespoon honey

Let each child mash the banana well. To mix the rest of the ingredients, let them put everything into a jar with a lid and shake, shake, shake! Provide spoons for them to fish out the banana chunks as they drink their jungle joy drink. If desired, serve each child a few croutons to nibble with the drink. Ask them to form Js with the croutons.

Other taste experiences for letter J: juices and jellyrolls.

SONGS AND POEMS

Song: "Jingle J"

(tune of "Jingle Bells")

Jingle J, jingle J, jingle jingle J. *(pretend to ring a bell)*
Oh what fun it is to jingle, jingle J today.

Other verses: Substitute *jumping/jump, juggling/juggle,* and *jiggling/jiggle jingle.*
Actions: For *jumping,* jump while singing; for *jiggling,* jiggle body while singing; for *juggling,* pretend to juggle.

Poem: "Jump Rope Jingle"

I asked my mother for fifty cents
To see an elephant jump over a fence.
He jumped so high, he reached the sky,
And didn't come back 'til the Fourth of July! *(jump rope to meter of poem)*
(If the children are not able to jump rope to jingles yet, let them jump without rope to the rhythm of the jingle.)

Poem: "Jumping, Jumping"

Jumping, jumping, one! two! three! *(jump in place)*
Jumping, jumping, look at me!

Jogging, jogging, one! two! three! *(jog in place)*
Jogging, jogging, look at me!

Jetting, jetting, one! two! three! *(hold arms out and move about like jet planes)*
Jetting, jetting, look at me!

JIFFY JETS

Teacher Directions: Cut out and color a "jet stream" for each player. Attach a spinner by inserting a brass fastener through a large paper clip and into the center of the wheel gameboard. Cut out the additional shapes for matching to the trails left by the jets. You can color these too.

Student Directions: Choose a jet stream. Take turns spinning the spinner. Match the shape that the spinner points to with the same shape on your jet stream and cover that shape. Try to cover your whole jet stream.

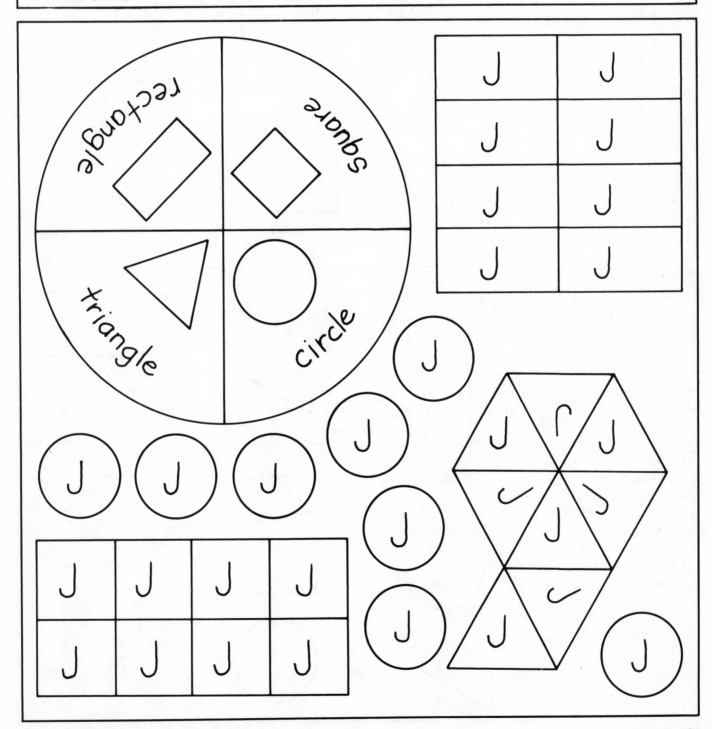

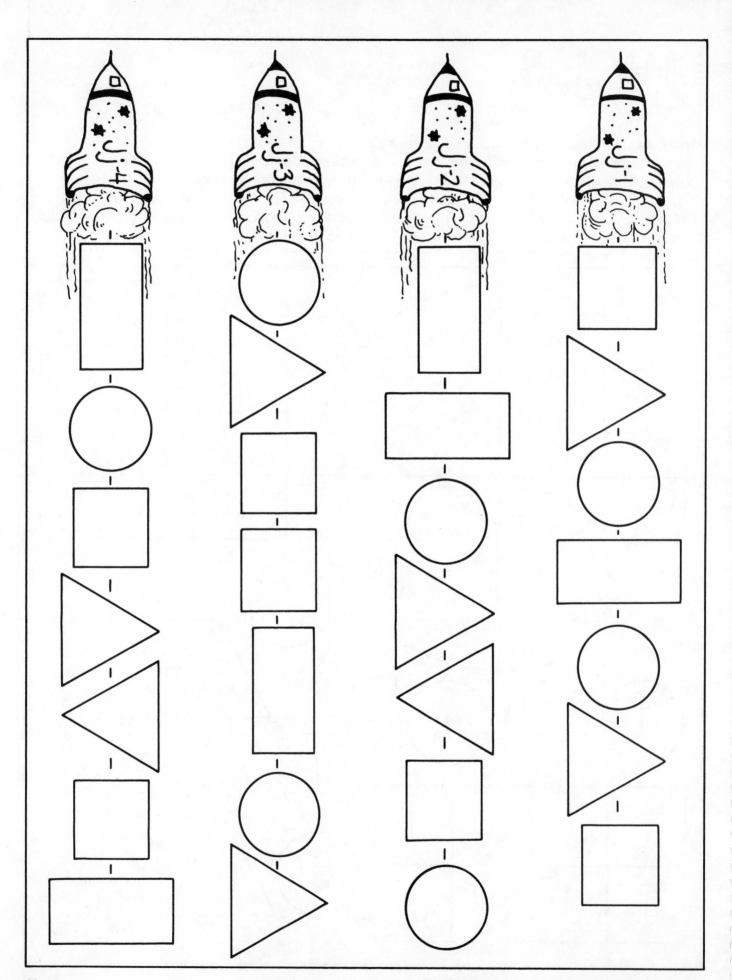

MOVEMENTS

Kittens

Let the children pretend to move like kittens. Tell them to first lay flat on their stomachs on the floor with their hands at their sides. Tell them to move their hands so that they are under their shoulders. They push themselves up onto their knees and lower their bottoms to their heels. Tell them to touch their foreheads to the floor. Ask them to stretch like a kitten and straighten themselves up. Let them repeat this stretching exercise slowly several times.

Kooky Kangaroos

Ask the children to pretend to be kangaroos by jumping around the play area. Vary this activity by asking them to take long jumps, short jumps, backward jumps, and sideways jumps. Ask them to link arms with a friend and kangaroo-jump together for a while.

Kicking Objects

Provide the children with a variety of objects to kick. Ask them to practice kicks in two different ways: Place the object to be kicked on the floor and kick it, then hold the object in one hand and kick it as it drops. Some things to use for kicking are balls of different sizes, beanbags, boxes, wadded newspaper, lids from plastic bowls, and small blocks.

Kernels

Ask the children to all pretend to be in a large pan. Tell them to each be a kernel of popcorn. Walk among them and tap them to indicate that they can begin to pop. They begin popping (jumping up and down) slowly at first and then faster and faster. When everyone has had time to pop, they may roll away in an area designated as the big popcorn bowl.

Kite Flying

Tell the children to find an open space on the play area. Ask them to pretend that they are flying kites on a windy day. Encourage them to stretch themselves up as high as possible. Let them run around pretending to move their kites along. Remind them to be careful not to bump into other kite fliers. When you have finished this activity, let the children lay in small groups on the floor, forming kite shapes. When the children have had time to cool down, ask each quiet group to "fly" to the next activity.

GAMES

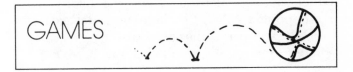

Kangaroo Relay

For this relay, ask the children to pretend that they are kangaroos with pouches. Provide beanbags or blocks for them to carry in their pouches (on their stomachs). Divide the group into teams. The team members will race across the floor on hands and feet, with their stomachs in the air and the objects perched on their stomachs. If the objects fall off during the race, they should stop and put the objects back onto their stomachs. Ask them to say **K** to the next person on their team when they have completed their part of the race.

K Beanbag Toss

Tape a large sheet of paper to the floor. Draw four or five big circles on it. In each circle, make a **K** and a number. Let the children take turns tossing beanbags into the circles. Tell them to keep track of the points they get by counting out kernels of unpopped corn. At the end of the game, ask all children to count their kernels. This is an excellent game to play in small groups so that children can have more turns.

Kicking Relay

Give each child or group of children a ball. Let them practice kicking it and running after it. Tell them to kick the balls back and forth with you and their friends. Have a kicking relay. Divide the children up into teams. Let each team choose a **K** name. Tell them to kick and run with the ball to a designated line and then to kick it back, running along with the ball.

Kickball

Teach the children to play kickball. Divide the children into teams. Let them choose **K** names for the teams. Keep score on a large sheet of paper so the children can watch and help count the points. This game may be played in innings, stretched over several days.

Catch the Kittens

Tell the children to stand on a line on the play area or in the gym. Show them a line opposite them that they will be running to. Choose one child to be the parent cat. That child stands in the center of the play area. When you call "Catch the kittens!" the children run to the opposite goal line. Children who are tagged by the mother cat remain in the center and help catch other children during the next round of play.

ALPHABET SNACK

Kangaroo Krunch

> 2 quarts popped corn (unsalted)
> ¼ cup butter
> ¼ cup peanut butter

Heat the peanut butter and butter together and pour over popped corn. Let the children take turns stirring the mixture to coat it well. Allow the snack to cool. Then ask the children to try forming some letter **K**s before eating their Kangaroo Krunch. Variation: Substitute ¼ cup brown sugar for the peanut butter and prepare as above. Sprinkle with some cinnamon.

Other taste experiences for letter **K**: kale, kidney beans, kohlrabi, and kumquats.

SONGS AND POEMS

Song: "Here We Go Round the Letter *K*"

(tune of "Here We Go Round the Mulberry Bush")

Here we go round the letter **K**, the letter **K**, the letter **K**.
Here we go round the letter **K**, while we're in kindergarten (or "while we are in a kitchen").
*(lay a large paper **K** in the center of the circle and walk around it while singing)*

This is the way we like to kick, like to kick, like to kick.
This is the way we like to kick, while we're in kindergarten. *(kick feet into circle while singing)*

This is the way to be kangaroos, kangaroos, kangaroos.
This is the way to be kangaroos, while we're in kindergarten. *(jump while singing)*

This is the way we turn our keys, turn our keys, turn our keys.
This is the way we turn our keys, while we're in kindergarten. *(pretend to turn a key)*.

Poem: "Ten Baby Kangaroos"

Ten baby kangaroos standing in a row. *(hold up ten fingers)*
When they see their mama, they bow just so. *(bend fingers up and down)*
They kick to the left, and they kick to the right. *(move hands left and right)*
Then they close their eyes and sleep all night. *(pretend to sleep)*

Other verses: Repeat the poem, going down a number each time—that is, begin each successive verse with "Nine baby kangaroos," "Eight baby kangaroos," and so on.

Poem: "Baby Kangaroo"

Jump, jump, jump goes the big kangaroo. *(make jumping motion with index finger, other fingers, and folded thumb)*
I thought there was one, but I see there are two. *(hold up one finger, then two)*
The mother takes her young one along in a pouch. *(index finger of left hand comes up between thumb and fingers of right hand)*
So he can take a rest like a kid on a couch. *(rest head on folded hands)*
Jump, jump, jump.
Jump, jump, jump. *(repeat jumping motion)*
Jump, jump, jump.

Other verses: Repeat the poem with the word *kick* in place of *jump.*

KIDDIE KONG

Teacher Directions: Color the gameboard. Cut out the game pieces and color each a different color. Glue them onto tiny blocks (optional). Cut out the octagon. Stick a pencil through the center to make a top.

Student Directions: Choose a marker and place it on Start. Take turns spinning the top. Go the number of spaces the spinner shows. Look at the spinner part closest to the ground—the number, letter, or face will be right side up. If you get a sad face, you lose your turn. If you get a **K**, you get another turn. See if you can get to the bananas first!

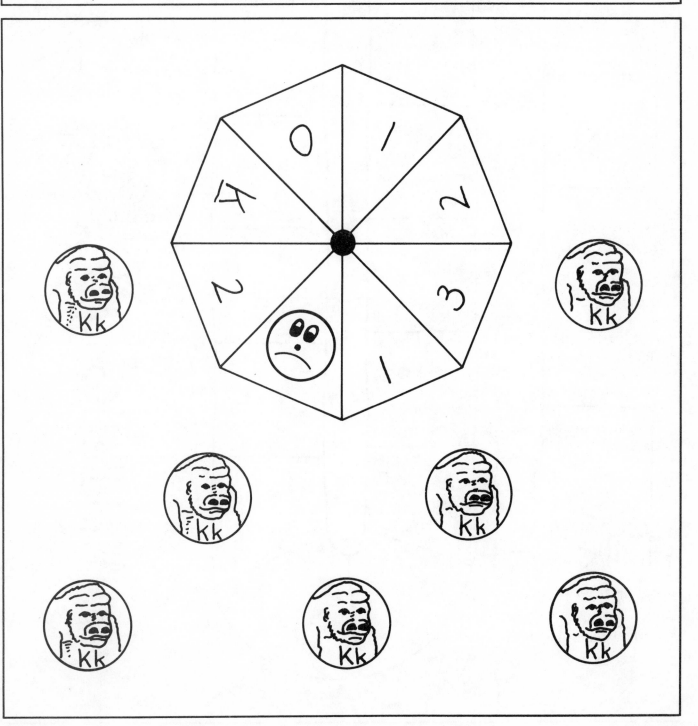

START

Kk

FINISH

Kiddie Kong

Ll

MOVEMENTS

Lying Around

Ask the children to lie down on the floor of the play area. Have them pretend they are things that lie flat such as a road that cars drive on, grass with a ladybug crawling over it, a sidewalk with a bicycle riding on it, and a river running through a valley with a boat sailing along on it. Let the children tell you how these things might feel. Encourage them to really use their imaginations during this exercise.

Log Rolls

Ask the children to do some log rolls along a mat or other soft surface. When they understand how to do the log roll, ask them to hold a ball in their hands above their heads and roll while holding the ball.

Ladybugs on a Ladder

Provide a ladder for this small-group activity. Ask the children to perform these movements as ladybugs:

- Jump through the sections as the ladder is held on its side
- Crawl in and out of the sections as the ladder lies on its side
- Crawl around the ladder as it lies flat
- Form a line by holding the shoulders of the person in front and stepping between the rungs of the ladder lying flat on the ground

Lobsters

Show the children a picture of a lobster. Let them talk about how it might feel to be a lobster. Let them pretend to act like lobsters, moving and stretching out their arms and legs as if to snap at something. Tell them to make words that have the **L** sound.

Lions

Ask the children to pretend to be fierce, ferocious lions prowling around the jungle. Let them roar at each other. Ask them to run as lions would. Tell the lions to walk backward as if afraid of a larger animal. Play some music to accompany movement. When the music stops, let the lions rest awhile.

Lines

Provide a "line" for each child. This can be a piece of string, some yarn, or a jump rope. Ask the children to lay their lines out on the play area. Direct them to perform some of these actions with their lines: jump over it, walk on it, walk around it, hop on it, hop over it, stand on the end, scissor-jump it, stretch out on it, roll over it, slide along it, tiptoe around it, lie beside it, skip around it, walk backward around it, crawl backward around it, run around it, pick it up and jump rope with it.

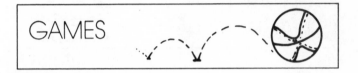

GAMES

Lake Game

Make a circle on the floor with tape, chalk, or string. The circle represents a lake. Make some paper fish for the lake. Put a couple staples in each fish and place the fish in the lake. Make some fishing poles from sticks, using string for lines and magnets for hooks. Let the children take turns standing around the lake to fish. Make this a more academic game by writing numbers, letters, or words on the fish for the children to read.

Who Is the Leader?

Ask the children to sit in a circle. Send one child from the room. Choose another child to be the leader. That child leads the group in performing a number of activities such as clapping, stamping, humming, bending, swaying, and clicking fingers. When the child from outside comes back in, he or she must decide who the leader is by watching who begins the motions.

Little Lost Lamb

Ask the children to sit in a circle. They are the lambs. Choose one child to leave the room. Choose another child to be removed from the circle of lambs. Let the lambs rearrange themselves in the circle as the "lost lamb" hides somewhere out of sight. Tell the child waiting outside to return, and ask him or her to identify the little lost lamb. Give all children a turn to be the lost lamb and the child to guess.

Lollipop Game

Make some lollipops out of colored paper and popsicle sticks. Mark them with letters, words, or numbers that you are teaching. Make about seven or eight for this game. Ask the children to stand in a circle. Choose one child to "sell" the lollipops. That person goes up to someone in the circle and says "Lollipop, lollipop, would you like a lollipop?" The child answers, "Yes, I would like _____" (naming a letter, number, or word). The lollipop salesperson finds the correct lollipop. The child who answered the question then takes over as the seller. Tell the children to sit down after they have had a turn. Play until everyone has had a turn.

ALPHABET SNACK

Ladybugs on a Log

Provide a small ripe banana or part of a larger one for each child. The banana represents a log. Show them how to stick sunflower seeds all over the banana to represent ladybugs. Or let them dip the banana in some wheat germ before eating it. Ask them to make the shape of the letter **L** with some of the sunflower seeds. Variations: Use chunks of cheese instead of bananas or try chopped peanuts instead of sunflower seeds.

Other taste experiences for letter **L**: lasagne, lemonade, lettuce, and limes.

SONGS AND POEMS

Song: "Looby Loo for *L*"

(tune of "Looby Loo")

Chorus: Let's go looby loo, let's go looby lie.
Let's go looby loo, all for the letter **L**. *(join hands and move in circle)*

We lift the ladder up, we lift the ladder up.
We lift the ladder up, up, up, and then we lay it down.
    (make lifting motion, then lowering motion for last line) (repeat chorus)

We lick our lollipops, we lick our lollipops.
We lick, lick, lick our lollipops, and then we lay them down. *(pretend to lick lollipops, then lower them for last line) (repeat chorus)*

We leap like lions, we leap like lions.
We leap, leap, leap like lions, and then we all lie down.
    (do leaping motion, then lie down for last line) (repeat chorus)

Poem: "Leo the Lion"

Leo the lion is the king of the jungle,
And his jaws are big and wide. ROAR!
Leo the lion, when he roars it's a warning
That you'd better run away and hide. ROAR!

Poem: "Mr. Lion and Mr. Lamb"

Mr. Lion took a walk one day *(make index finger of right hand walk in front of self)*
In a very fine way.
Along came Mr. Lamb. *(index finger of left hand walks to meet lion)*
Roar roar roar! *(wiggle right index finger)*
Baa baa baa! *(wiggle left index finger)*
Goodbye, goodbye. *(bow with right, then left, index fingers)*
And they both walked away on that very fine day.
    (make fingers go behind self)

LOOPY LOOPS

Teacher Directions: Duplicate the loop page in red, blue, green, and yellow. Cut out the loops and fold them on the dotted lines. Make the spinner by inserting a brass fastener through a large paper clip into the center of the square. Color the square.

Student Directions: Place all of the loops in the middle of your group. Choose a color. Take turns spinning the spinner. If you spin your color, take a loop of that color. If you do not get your color, pass the spinner to the next player. Each time you spin your color, take another loop, push it through the center of the last loop, and fold it over to form a chain. The first player to have five loops on a chain is the winner.

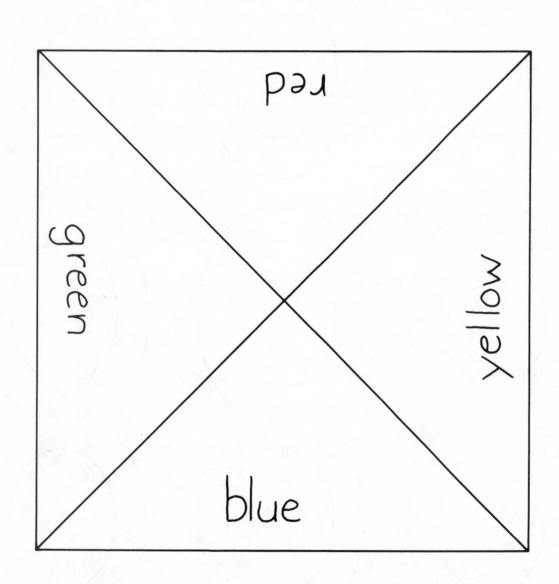

Mm

MOVEMENTS

Mice

Let the children pretend to be mice. Ask them to get down on hands and knees and crawl around. Provide some things for the mice to crawl through such as hoops, boxes with both ends cut out, or tables. Ask them to try to crawl backward and forward. Tell them to stretch out various body parts—right front paw, left front paw, right back paw, and left back paw. Ask them to pretend to find and eat bits of cheese and say "Mmmmmmmm!"

Movements

Work with many kinds of movements: standing, swaying, oozing, drooping, stooping, skipping, sliding, jumping, bending, sitting, rocking, squatting, spreading, stretching, leaping, hopping, twirling, running, swinging, lying, rolling, galloping, kneeling, flopping, crawling, squiggling, and slithering. Encourage the children to give ideas for each of these movements. Talk with the children about how wonderful our bodies are because they are able to do so many things.

Monster Mash

Play some spooky music and ask the children to pretend they are doing the latest monster dance, the Monster Mash. Tell them to make mashing movements with their feet during the dance. Every once in a while, they can greet other monsters with the sound of letter **M**.

Monkey Jumps

Give each child a jump rope. Have them put their ropes on the floor and shape them to represent trees in the jungle. Ask the children to pretend they are monkeys beside their trees. Have the children imitate monkeys swinging from tree to tree. As they travel to other rope-trees on the floor, the children should take long smooth steps and swing their arms widely. Tell

them to jump in and out of their trees, reciting this verse as they do so:

> Monkey business is my game
> Jumping, jumping is my fame
> How many times can I jump?
> One, two, three, four . . .

Ask the children to pick up their ropes and to practice jumping. Have them recite the jingle as they jump rope the conventional way.

GAMES

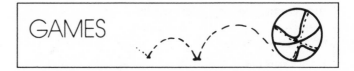

Man From Mars

Ask the children to stand on a goal line in the play area. Choose someone to be the Man from Mars, who then stands a short distance from them. Teach the children to call out, "Man from Mars, can we chase you to the stars?" Tell the Man from Mars to say, "Yes, if you are wearing _____" (a color). All children wearing that color try to chase the Man from Mars. The first person who tags the Man from Mars becomes the next Man from Mars. Adapt this game by using letters in the children's names instead of colors.

Midnight

Choose one child to be the fox and another to be the hen. All the other children are the chickens. Tell the hen and the chickens to stand on a line in the play area about 30 feet away from where the fox is standing. The hen leads her chickens to the fox and asks, "What time it is, old fox?" The fox answers different times, but when the fox says "Midnight!" the hen and her chickens run away. The fox tries to catch them by tagging them on the shoulder. Anyone the fox tags must help catch the remaining chickens during the next rounds of the game. Play until all but one of the chickens is tagged. That person can be the fox for the next game.

Mail Carrier

Ask the children to sit in a circle on the floor. Give them a large ball. Teach them to say, "I'm mailing a letter to _____" (name another child in the circle), then to roll the ball to that child. Encourage them to give everyone a turn. After one round, ask them to stand up and toss the ball, repeating the same message and calling out each player's name in turn. For the last round of the game, ask them to stand facing outside the circle and to mail their "letters" backward through their legs.

The Mitten Game

Bring two pairs of mittens for this race. Divide the group into two equal teams and line them up so the teams are facing each other. Give the first person on each team a pair of mittens. On the signal "**M**", the children must put on the pair of mittens, take them off, and hand them to the next player. When the last player has the mittens on, that team is finished. Whoever finishes first is the winner.

The Mousetrap Game

Choose someone to be the mouse. Ask the rest of the children to hold hands, forming a circle to represent the mousetrap. Tell the mouse to go inside the trap. Teach the children to say, "One, two, three, four, five, I caught a mouse alive. Six, seven, eight, nine, ten, I let it go again." At the word "ten," the children in the circle hold their hands up in arches. The mouse tries to escape before the children put their arms down again on the words "go again." Let each mouse choose someone to take his or her place for the next game.

Musical Letters

Ask the children to sit in a circle. Let them pass a beanbag around the circle while you play some music. When the music stops, whoever is holding the beanbag goes to the center of the circle, takes a picture card, and tells what letter it begins with. Use cards for any concept you are studying—letters, sounds, numbers, words, shapes, and so on.

ALPHABET SNACK

Monkey Favorite

For each child, provide half of a banana, thinly sliced. Carefully drop the banana slices into an electric skillet with a layer of heated oil. Fry until light brown, turn them over, and fry the other side. Drain on paper towels. When cool, let the children lay some in the shape of the letter **M** before eating the bananas. They can also put the bananas on slices of whole wheat bread to make sandwiches! Ask them to make the sound of **M** after eating: "Mmmmmm!"

Other taste experiences for letter **M**: macaroni, meatloaf, melba toast, Mozzarella cheese, muffins, and mushrooms.

SONGS AND POEMS

Song: "I Am a Monster"

(tune of "On Top of Old Smokey")

Oh, I am a monster. *(make a scary face)*
I went to the moon. *(point up)*
I found letter **M**, *(form **M** with fingers pointed downward)*
M-m-m-m-m. *(Sound of **M**)*

Other verses: Substitute *manhole, meadow, mirror,* and *mountain* for *moon.*
Actions: For *manhole,* make circles around eyes looking down; for *meadow,* spread arms outward; for *mirror,* pretend to look at self in mirror; for *mountain,* draw an imaginary mountain in the air.

Poem: "Me"

Ten little fingers, ten little toes.
Two little eyes, one little nose.
Put them all together, and what have you got?
You've got ME, and that's a lot. *(have children point to body parts as they are mentioned)*

Poem: "My Mother"

I have a wonderful mother, a mother who never grows old. *(shake head from side to side)*
She has a smile of sunshine. She has a heart of gold. *(for smile, put pointing fingers by mouth; for heart, hold hands over heart)*
She is as much like an angel as anyone ever could be. *(pretend to flutter hands at shoulders)*
I have a wonderful mother, and my mother belongs to ME! *(point to self)*

Poem: "Mother Dear"

Mother Dear, can you guess *(put hands on hips)*
Who it is that loves you best? *(hold arms out with palms up)*
I'll give you three guesses, one, two, three. *(hold up three fingers; point to them as you count)*
There! I knew you'd think of me! *(nod head up and down and point to self)*

MONKEY BUSINESS

Teacher Directions: Color and cut out the monkeys and the bananas. Punch out the holes. Tie a piece of yarn, string, or shoelace about 12 inches long around each monkey's tail.

Student Directions: Choose a monkey. Look at his funny tail! Help the monkey carry things on his tail by finding pictures on the bananas that rhyme with the picture on his tummy. String the pictures on his tail.

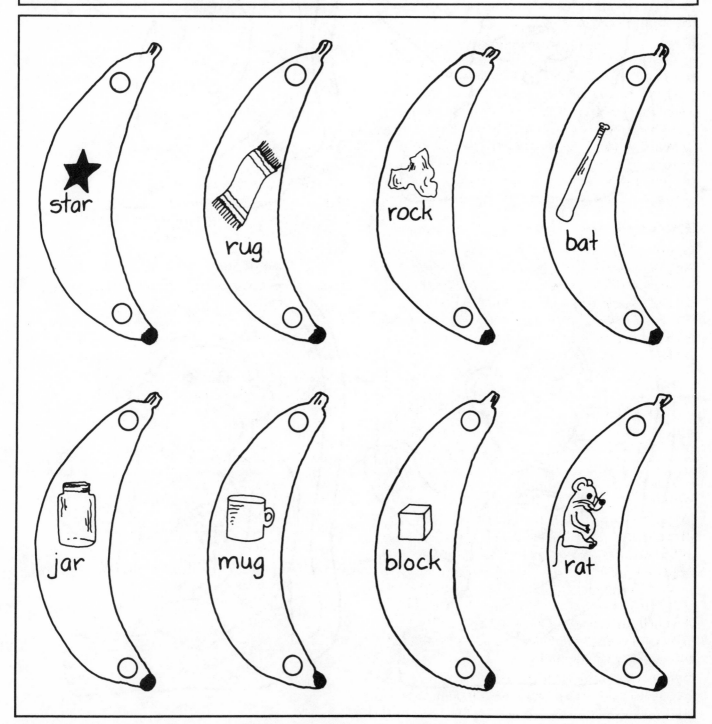

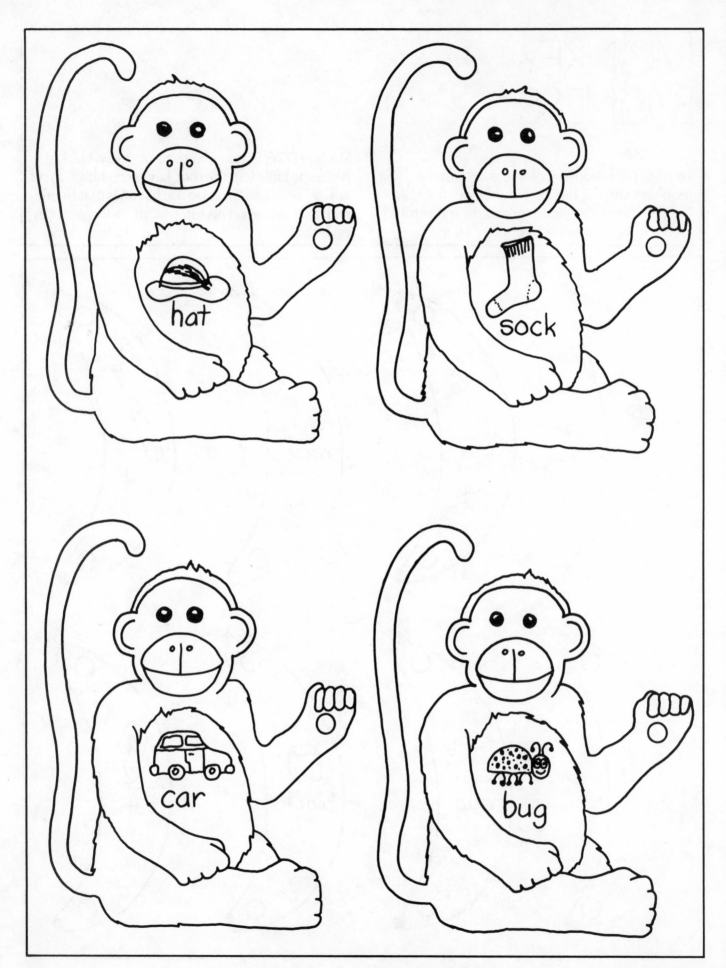

hat

sock

car

bug

Nn

MOVEMENTS

Newspaper News

Give each child a sheet of newspaper. Ask the children to perform some of these actions with the newspaper: sit on it, jump around it; get under it; use it as wings; throw it up in the air and catch it; make a fort and get in it; crawl around it; crawl under it; crunch it up, then throw the crunched-up ball of newspaper, and pretend to have a snowball fight; pretend the newspaper balls are leaves, and rake up the leaves and jump in them.

Nap Time!

Call out movements for the children to perform in a large area. They must also listen for a whistle and the signal "Nap Time" and freeze when they hear the signal. Call out movements such as walking backward, bear walking, elephant walking, tiptoeing, walking heel-to-toe, running, galloping, and skipping.

Noises

Ask the children to make all kinds of different noises with their bodies, without using their voices. Examples might be clapping, stomping, rubbing hands, and so on. Encourage them to try all the ideas that are named. Have a noise band. Choose a song everyone likes and sing it as the children make body noises to the beat.

Nests

Give each child a jump rope or a piece of string to form a nest on the play area. Ask the children to pretend they are nightingales. Call out "In" and "Out." They must respond by hopping in and out of their nests. Ask them to lay their nests out in a line. Tell them to hop around the line first on the right foot and then on the left foot. Ask them to hop backward around the line on each foot.

Newt Movements

Bring a picture of a newt to show the group. Ask the children to pretend to be newts. Tell them to talk, making only the sound of the letter **N**. Tell the newts to try to slither backward. Ask them to roll over onto their right sides and then their left sides.

GAMES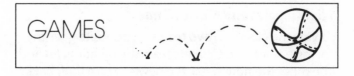

N Necklace

Prepare a string necklace with a lettercard **N** strung on it. Tell the children to stand in a circle. Choose one child to stand in the center and begin the game, wearing the necklace and giving a word having the sound of **N**. That child then takes off the necklace and gives it to someone else standing in the circle. That child then goes to the center of the circle, puts on the necklace, and gives a new **N** word. The game continues until everyone has had a turn. Ask the children to sit down after they have had a turn.

Newspaper Toss

Give each child a piece of newspaper to crumple up. Divide the class into teams. Show them how to throw their papers into empty boxes or wastebaskets. Count the number of successful "baskets" for each team. Record the numbers for the children to see. Play a number of rounds of this game.

Needle Game

Line the children up in a column. Ask the children to hold onto the hand of the person in front of them and the person in back of them. Tell them that together they are a piece of thread. Choose two children to be the needle, and have them stand as an arch for everyone to walk through. Teach the children this song to sing as they play:

> Through the needle we will go,
> We will go, we will go.
> Through the needle we will go
> For letter **N**. *(tune of "London Bridge")*

Once the children understand this procedure, choose more pairs for needles so that the rest of the children can go through a succession of needles. Give everyone a chance to be part of a needle.

Nose and Neck Tag

Teach the children how to play tag. Then explain that they are safe from being tagged if, just before "It" touches the person, the person quickly puts a finger on his or her own nose and a finger on his or her own neck. If you would like, divide them into smaller groups for this activity.

Nightingales and Newts Game

Divide the class into two teams on opposite goal lines facing each other. Call one team the nightingales and the other the newts. Ask the newts to turn their backs to the nightingales, then tell the nightingales to tiptoe up to the newts very quietly while the newts are facing away. Call out, "The nightingales are here!" The newts then chase the nightingales back to their goal line. Tagged players become part of the newt team. Next, the newt team tiptoes up to the nightingales, and the game is replayed.

ALPHABET
SNACK

Oodles of Noodles

Show the children what uncooked noodles look like. Let each child feel one. Ask them if they can form the letter **N** with one. Cook a package of noodles for the children according to package directions. Serve a small helping for each child and let them stir in a little butter and some sesame seeds. Ask them to try to make the letter **N** now that the noodles are soft. Try to serve a nutritious noodle such as whole wheat or spinach ones.

Other taste experiences for letter **N**: nuts and nectarines.

SONGS
AND POEMS

Song: "Ns in the Nest"

(tune of "Skip to My Lou")
Ns in the nest now, what'll I do?
Ns in the nest now, what'll I do?
Ns in the nest now, what'll I do?
I'll go n (sound of N) for **N** now. (make a nest with hands)

Nail the **N**s now, that's what I'll do.
Nail the **N**s now, that's what I'll do.
Nail the **N**s now, that's what I'll do.
I'll go n for **N** now. (pretend to pound a nail)
Needle the **N**s now, that's what I'll do.
Needle the **N**s now, that's what I'll do.
Needle the **N**s now, that's what I'll do.
I'll go n for **N** now. (pretend to sew)
Net the **N**s now, that what I'll do.
Net the **N**s now, that's what I'll do.
Net the **N**s now, that's what I'll do.
I'll go n for **N** now. (pretend to catch something in a net)

Poem: "Here's a Nest"

Here's a nest for robin redbreast. (cup hands)
Here's a hive for busy bee. (clench fist)
Here's a hole for jacky-rabbit. (thumb around forefinger)
And here's a house for me! (fingers together forming the roof of a house)

Poem: "Nibble, Nibble"

Nibble, nibble little newts. (rub thumb and forefinger together)
Run into your nest. (make fingers run along arm)
Look to see if you can find (hold hand above eyes)
Where nibbling is the best. (rub stomach after another nibbling motion)

THE NAME GAME

Student Directions: Find a container with the name and picture of an **N** word on it. Can you make the word? Take out the letters. Put them in order to make the word.

n	a	i	l	s	n	u
m	b	e	r	s	n	e
s	t	n	i	n	e	n
u	t	s	n	o	s	e
n	e	c	k	l	a	c
e	n	e	e	d	l	e

numbers

necklace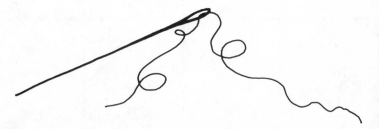

needle

nails  nine

nest  nose

nuts

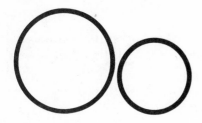

MOVEMENTS

Ostrich Walk

Show the children how to do the ostrich walk: Tell them to bend forward at the waist and grasp their ankles with their hands. Show them how to stretch their necks in and out as they walk. Tell them to keep their eyes open very wide.

Obstacle Course

Set up an obstacle course for the children to go through. Use some or all of these things: a tunnel; boxes with ends cut out; hula hoops; a balance beam; jump ropes; mats on which the children can do log-rolls; a "tightrope" taped on the floor; a "river," taped on the floor, over which the children can bear-walk without touching; and a bar to crawl under. Use some pieces of colored tape to mark the path you want the children to follow on the obstacle course.

Over the Rope

Choose two children to hold the ends of a rope. Tell the other children to form a line and jump over the rope. After they jump, they return to the end of the line. Let the children holding the rope lift it a little higher each time the children take a turn. Another "over the rope" activity is to lay a number of ropes out across the floor. Let the children hop over all of them, one at a time.

Ovals

Show the children something that has the shape of an oval. Talk about that shape. Ask the children to name things that are found in that shape. Tell them to try to form their bodies into an oval shape. Let them work in groups of two and three and later as a class oval.

Olympics

Set up four or five centers in the play area for this activity. Some activities for the Olympics might be long jumping, high jumping, running races such as sack races, jumping rope, and making baskets. Enlist the help of parents or older children. Divide the children into small groups and let them attend each event in the Olympics. Let them test their skills. Give out ribbons for everyone who is a good sport.

Orchestra Time

Talk with the children about what an orchestra is. Show them a picture if possible. Tell them about the conductor and how that person keeps everyone together with directing. Explain to the children that they can be an orchestra too. You will be the conductor. This orchestra will be with body movements instead of music. Tell the children to stand on a line opposite you. Using your hands, direct them to come forward or to go backward or sideways by beckoning, pointing, and making other hand motions. Let the children try to be conductors too. The fun of this game is that no one talks, but everyone still knows what they are supposed to do.

Octopus in the Ocean

Tell the children to pretend they are all octopuses in the ocean, swimming around, sitting on rocks, and making the sound of short **O.** Try to form a class octopus using eight children for the legs and the rest for the body.

GAMES

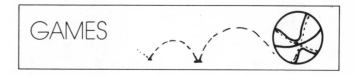

The *O* Game

Cut out a cardboard oval with a hole in the middle large enough to see a child's face. Ask the children to stand in a circle. Choose someone to go to the middle of the circle and begin the game by calling "**O, O,** _____" (call a child's name) while looking at the person he or she is calling through the **O.** Then the child who is called comes to the center of the circle to repeat this procedure, naming a different child. Play until everyone has had a turn. Ask the children to sit down after they have had a turn. Play the game a second time and have the children call the sound of short **O** and the child's name instead of the name of the letter. They might also give a word with the sound of short **O**.

Order, Order!

Give each child a different number card to hold. Tell the children to perform some moving action such as walking, running, hopping, skipping, or galloping. When you call "Order, Order!" they must rush to a designated line and arrange themselves in numerical order. Ask them to exchange numbers. Call out a different motion for each game round.

Over the Ocean

This is a game to be played in a gym or on a large outdoor area. Mark boundaries for the game and be sure to point them out to the children. Explain that the children are fish in the ocean and that they swim from one side of the ocean to the other by running. Choose one child to be an octopus who will try to catch the fish. When the octopus calls, "Over the ocean!" the fish run from one goal line to an opposite one. The octopus stands in the middle of the area and runs around trying to catch the fish before they reach the other line. Any fish the octopus catches must stop in mid-ocean right where it was tagged, and it must remain frozen there. The frozen fish can help the octopus tag other children, but only by moving their arms. Only the octopus is allowed to catch others by running. Fish who swim outside the boundaries will also become frozen. The game continues until all but one child is tagged. That child becomes the octopus for the next game.

ALPHABET
SNACK

Oh, Pineapp-*O*!

Serve each child a slice of canned pineapple. Talk about its shape. Let each child build another **O** on the pineapple **O** using some of the following ingredients: raisins, a variety of nuts, sunflower seeds, cut-up fruits, vegetable bits, and Cheerios.

Other taste experiences for letter **O**: oatmeal, oranges, orange juice, olives, and omelets.

SONGS
AND POEMS

Song: "Ten Little *O*s"

(tune of "Ten Little Indians")

One little, two little, three little **O**s.
Four little, five little, six little **O**s.
Seven little, eight little, nine little **O**s.
Ten little **O**s in the ocean. *(put up fingers as you count and sing)*

Ŏ-ŏ-ŏ-ŏ-ŏ say the **O**s (sound of short **O**).
Ŏ-ŏ-ŏ-ŏ-ŏ say the **O**s.
Ŏ-ŏ-ŏ-ŏ-ŏ say the **O**s.
Ten little **O**s in the ocean. *(make fingers **O**s)*

The **O**s go see an octopus.
The **O**s go see an octopus.
The **O**s go see an octopus.
Ten little **O**s in the ocean. *(make swimming motion with hands)*

The **O**s go see an old, old owl.
The **O**s go see an old, old owl.
The **O**s go see an old, old owl.
Ten little **O**s in the ocean. *(make circles around eyes with fingers)*

Poem: "Open Them, Shut Them"

Open them, shut them, open them, shut them, give a little clap.
Open them, shut them, open them, shut them, lay them in your lap.
Creep them, crawl them, creep them, crawl them, right up to your chin.
Creep them, crawl them, creep them, crawl them, but do not let them in.
Creep them, crawl them, creep them, crawl them, right up to your cheek.
Open wide your little eyes, and through those fingers peek! *(make **O**s around eyes)*

Poem: "Three *O*s"

Here's an **O**, *(make an **O** with thumb and forefinger)*
And here's an **O**, *(make an **O** with hands together)*
And a great big **O** you see. *(make an **O** with arms)*
Can you count them?
Are you ready?
One! Two! Three! *(repeat each **O**)*

OLGA OCTOPUS

Teacher Directions: Color and cut out the octopus and the eight objects she is to hold. Put them in a folder.

Student Directions: Help Olga Octopus hold all her belongings. Match each object to the arm with the correct beginning letter. If you are right, the piece will fit on like a puzzle.

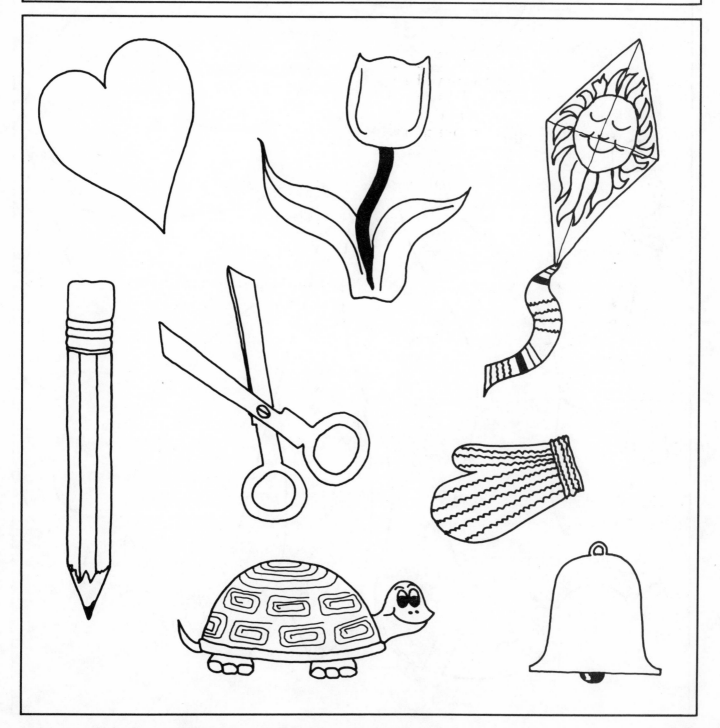

MOVEMENTS

Piece of Paper

Ask the children to lie down flat on the floor. Ask each child to pretend being a piece of paper. Play some music very softly. Tell the children that the music is the wind. They could imagine that when they hear the soft music, the wind is blowing gently so they can get up and move around a little. As the music get louder, the wind is blowing harder, and the children begin to move faster and faster. When the music stops, the wind is gone and they once again must lie flat.

Paper Plates

Give each child a sturdy paper plate to use as a Frisbee. Print a capital and a lower-case **P** on each plate. Let the children throw and catch the Frisbees, balance them on their heads while walking, and hold them between their legs at the knees while trying to walk and run.

Penguins

Show the children how to make penguin movements and let them pretend to move around as peppy penguins. Show them how to hold their arms close to their sides with hands pointing out. They must walk with legs very close together. Ask the children to greet each other with the sound of the letter **P.**

Parade

Let each child choose an animal or some other type of character for a parade. Play some parade music and let the children march around doing their tricks. Invite another class to come and watch the parade and later join in. Let the children make and carry flags with the letter **Pp** printed on the flags. They might use straws for flag holders.

Parachute Play

Position the children in your class around a parachute. Tell them to hold onto it using an overhand grasp. Direct the following movements, making sure the children understand the importance of listening and following directions during this activity:

- Walk to the right and left while holding the parachute.
- Run to the right and left.
- Skip to the right and left.
- Do sit-ups while holding onto the edges.
- Shake the parachute to make ripples and waves.
- Put balls on the parachute as popcorn and make them "pop."
- Pull it up as high as possible to make a mountain.
- Call out motions "Up, "Down," "Up," "Down," and "Let go!" Tell children to step back and watch what happens.
- Call out motions "Up," "Down," "Up," "Down," and "Get under!" Tell children to crawl under the parachute and let it fall on them.
- Have tug-of-wars with it after it is rolled up.
- Let the children take turns exchanging places around the parachute by running under it as it is held. Call out two or three names at a time.

If you are unable to get a parachute, use an old sheet or light bedspread with a smaller group of children.

Pat and Bounce

Give each child or pair of children a ball to work with. Let them practice bouncing balls. Tell them to practice using both their right and left hands to bounce. Encourage them to pat the ball while bouncing it.

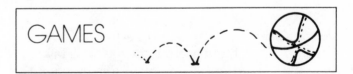

GAMES

Pillowcase Race

Provide some old pillowcases. Divide the group into teams. Show them how to crawl into the pillowcase and hop along. Let them race to a line and back again, calling "**P**" to the next racer.

Police Officer

Ask the children to form a circle. Choose someone to be the police officer. Describe someone who is "wanted" by the police. As the police officer listens to your description, the child being described realizes it and begins to run. The police officer tries to catch that player before he or she can get back to the original space left in the circle. If caught, the person described becomes the new police officer.

Pull, Pull, Pull!

Bring a very strong rope. Divide the children into two teams and put one at either end of the rope. Show them a line in the gym or on the play area. Tell them that they must pull the other team past the line. Use more ropes and smaller teams for this activity if you have more materials available.

Poison

Ask the children to form a circle with hands joined. Inside the circle, draw a second circle on the floor or playground about a foot in front of the children. With their hands joined, the children pull and tug each other trying to make someone step into the drawn circle, which is "poison." The first one to be poisoned becomes a chaser and chases all the children back to a designated safe area. Anyone who is caught becomes a chaser as well. The first chaser calls everyone back to the circle when everyone who hasn't been caught reaches the safe area. The chaser calls out "Please play Poison!" The game begins again.

ALPHABET SNACK

P-Tatoes

Provide a half of a small potato for each child. Show them how to scrub and peel the potatoes well. Talk about the feel and look of the potato in its raw state. Then cook the potatoes until very soft. Drain. Let the children take turns using a potato masher to mash the potatoes. Pour a little milk in as they are being mashed. Scoop the potatoes onto a serving tray in the shape of the letter **P.** Sprinkle with paprika and garnish with parsley sprigs.

Other taste experiences for letter **P**: pudding, pancakes, parsnips, peaches, peanuts, pears, popcorn, pineapple, plums, prunes, and pumpkin.

SONGS AND POEMS

Song: "The Pigs in the Park"

(tune of "The People on the Bus")

The pigs in the park go push-push-push, push-push-push, push-push-push *(make pushing motions away from self with hands)*
The pigs in the park go push-push-push, all around the petunia patch.

Other verses: Substitute *pow, peek, poke,* and *play* for *push.*
Actions: For *pow,* slam one hand into other fist; for *peek,* look through hands; for *poke,* put finger of one hand into the other palm; for *play,* move around in circle.

Poem: "Ten Little Peas"

Ten little peas in a pea pod pocket. *(hold closed hands together, hiding fingers)*
One grew, two grew, and then all the rest. *(move closed hands farther and farther apart as peas grow)*
They grew and they grew and they grew and they grew.
Then, one day, the pea pod POPPED! *(lower voice and clap hands on* popped*)*

PLAY THE PIGS

Teacher Directions: Duplicate a gameboard and set of number cards for each player. Color and cut out the gameboards. Cut out the number cards.

Student Directions: Shuffle the number cards. Put them in a stack with the numbers facing down. Lay the gameboard in front of you. Take one card at a time from the stack. First play the pig on the left: If the number on your card is greater than the pig's, you win the card. Put it in your pile. If the pig's number is greater, give the card to the pig pile. Next play the second pig, and so on. After the cards are all gone, count to see who won— you or the pigs?

1	2	3	4	5	6
7	8	9	10	11	12

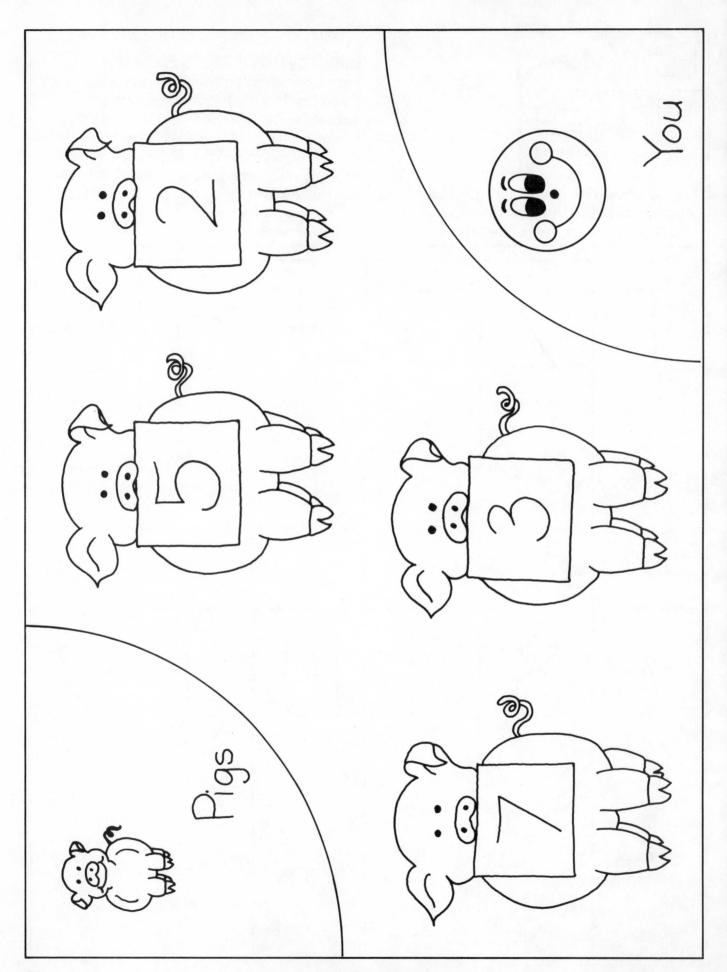

You

Pigs

MOVEMENTS

Quick-rope

Play this game with small groups of children. Occupy the rest of your class with bouncing balls, a game of catch, or some such activity. Hold one end of a rope and lay the other end on the floor. You will be the axis that turns the rope in a circular motion. Let the children try to jump over the rope quickly as it comes to them. The child should stay in the same place and jump each time the rope comes around. Tell the children they must be quick to watch and move.

Quick Bounce

Give each child a large ball to work with in the gym or in some other large area. Ask the children to practice bouncing the balls. Then ask them to try to clap their hands between bounces or before catching the ball. Then ask them to work in pairs, bouncing balls to their partners. Vary the motion between bounces or catches to other actions such as clapping knees, clicking fingers, and touching noses.

Quilts

Bring in some old sheets or blankets to use as quilts for this game. Spread them out on the play area with lots of space between them. Direct the children to perform some of these activities with the quilts:

1. Working in small groups, assign certain children to each quilt. Tell them to get *on* the quilt, *under* the quilt, and wrap themselves *in* the quilt. Have them hold the quilt along the sides and shake it up and down. Have the children move in circles with the quilt while running, walking, skipping, and hopping.

2. Play music to accompany running. When the music stops, the children must sit down on a quilt. Limit the number that can sit on each quilt.

3. Let small groups practice folding the quilts.
4. Play tug-of-war with the quilts.
5. Let the children take turns wrapping someone in a quilt and gently rolling the person along the floor.
6. Lay all the quilts together on the floor, making a giant bed. Ask all the children to come and pretend to have a quiet rest.

Quail

Read the children some interesting facts about the quail. Show them a picture of this bird. Ask them to pretend to be quail, flying about the play area. Ask them to make the sound of **Q** when they meet other quail.

Quarter-Backs

Divide the group into pairs. Ask them to sit back-to-back with their partners. Tell them to lock their arms together at the elbows. Explain that they are to have a race to see who can be first to push his or her partner over a designated line on the gym floor. The children must remain sitting or squatting.

Quackers

Ask the children to pretend to be ducks. Let them waddle all around the play area squatting down as they move about. Tell them to tuck their hands under their arms to make wings to flap. Let the quackers have a race from one end of the "barnyard" to the other.

GAMES

Quail Hunt

Choose one child to be the hunter. Tell this child to say to the other children, "Who would like to hunt quail with me?" The children get in a line behind the hunter and march around after him or her. When the hunter calls **Q,** the children run away. The hunter tries to tag someone, who then becomes the hunter for the next game.

Quiet, Please

Ask the children to sit in a circle facing in. Give each child a little square of paper with the letter **Q** written on it. Ask them to lay their letters on the floor in front of them. Go to the center of the circle and beckon to one of the children. That child brings his or her **Q**, comes to the center to take your place, and places the **Q** down. Then that child beckons to someone else, and the game continues. Play until all the **Q**s are in the center of the circle in the shape of the letter **Q**. This is a game during which no one has to make any sounds at all.

Listen for the *Quack*

Ask the children to stand around you in a large open area. Explain that you will tell them a story. Sometime during the telling you will say the word "quack." When you do so, they should begin to run away from you. You try to tag someone, who then begins the game again by telling another story. For example: Once upon a time there was a little boy who lived in a cottage in the forest. He was going for a walk one day when he "quack" . . .

Q-Tip Game

Divide the children into two equal teams. Give the members of one team five or six Q-tips each. Ask them to "hide" the Q-tips on themselves so only a small part of each swab is visible. Tell them to stand in a line. Assign one child from the team with the Q-tips to each member of the other team. The members of the other team must find all the Q-tips they can in a designated amount of time. Count to see who finds the most. Play the game again, reversing the roles. When the game is over, ask each pair of children to form a **Q** with all the Q-tips end-to-end.

ALPHABET SNACK

Queens With Crowns

Provide a half or a quarter apple for each child to use as the queen's face. Show them how to put the rounded side up. Let the children help cut up a variety of cut-up foods to use as "jewels" for the top of the crowns: cheese, bananas, pineapple, oranges, grapes, carrots, celery, and strawberries. Demonstrate how to build crowns: stick toothpicks into the apple, forming a line, and stick the cut-up foods onto the ends of the toothpicks. Let the children form the letter **Q** out of other cut-up fruit for their queens to look at.

Other taste experiences for letter **Q**: quiche and quinces.

SONGS AND POEMS

Song: "I've Got the Letter *Q*"

(tune of "He's Got the Whole World")

I've got the letter **Q** on my quilt. *(for* **Q***, make* **Q** *with fingers; for* quilt, *pretend to smooth out a quilt)*
I've got the letter **Q** on my quilt.
I've got the letter **Q** on my quilt, Q-q-q-q-q-q-q. *(sing the sound of* **Q** *throughout the song, clapping as you do so)*

Other verses: Substitute *quarter* and *quacker* for *quilt*. Actions: For *quarter*, pretend to hold a quarter by making a circle with thumb and forefinger; for *quacker*, make beak with hands.

Poem: "Quack, Quack"

Five little ducks went out to play,
Over the hill and far away. *(wave hand back for* far away)
Mother Duck called, "Quack, quack, quack." *(open thumb with fingers for* quack)
Four little ducks came waddling back. *(hold up number of fingers for number of ducks)*

Four little ducks went out to play,
Over the hill and far away,
Mother Duck called, "Quack, quack, quack."
Three little ducks came waddling back.

Three little ducks went out to play,
Over the hill and far away.
Mother Duck called, "Quack, quack, quack."
Two little ducks came waddling back.
(continue poem until none came back, *then add:)*
BUT, when Daddy Duck called, "QUACK QUACK QUACK," *(louder)*
Five little ducks came waddling back!

Poem: "Make a *Q*"

One, two, make a **Q** *(hold up one and two fingers; form* **Q** *with thumb and forefinger in a circle and forefinger of other hand making the tail)*
Three, four, make one more. *(hold up three and four fingers)*
Five, six, make one quick. *(hold up five and six fingers and then make* **Q** *quickly)*
Seven, eight, make one late. *(hold up seven and eight fingers and make* **Q** *slowly)*
Nine, ten, make **Q** again. *(hold up nine and ten fingers and make one last* **Q***)*

SLAP **Q**

Teacher Directions: Duplicate these letter cards on heavy paper. Cut them apart. Cover one side of them with clear contact paper so they look more like a deck of cards (optional). You may want to make two sets.

Student Directions: Sit in a circle. Pass out all of the cards. Keep them face down. Take turns flipping over and laying down one card at a time in the middle of the circle. Call out the letters on the cards as you lay them down. When you see a **Q** card, slap the pile. Whoever is the first to slap the **Q** gets the stack of cards. See who can get the biggest stack of cards!

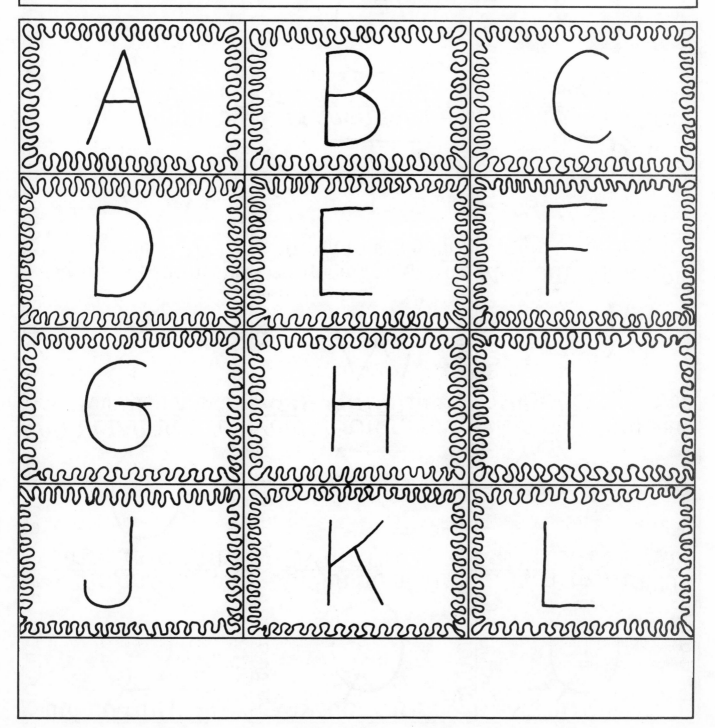

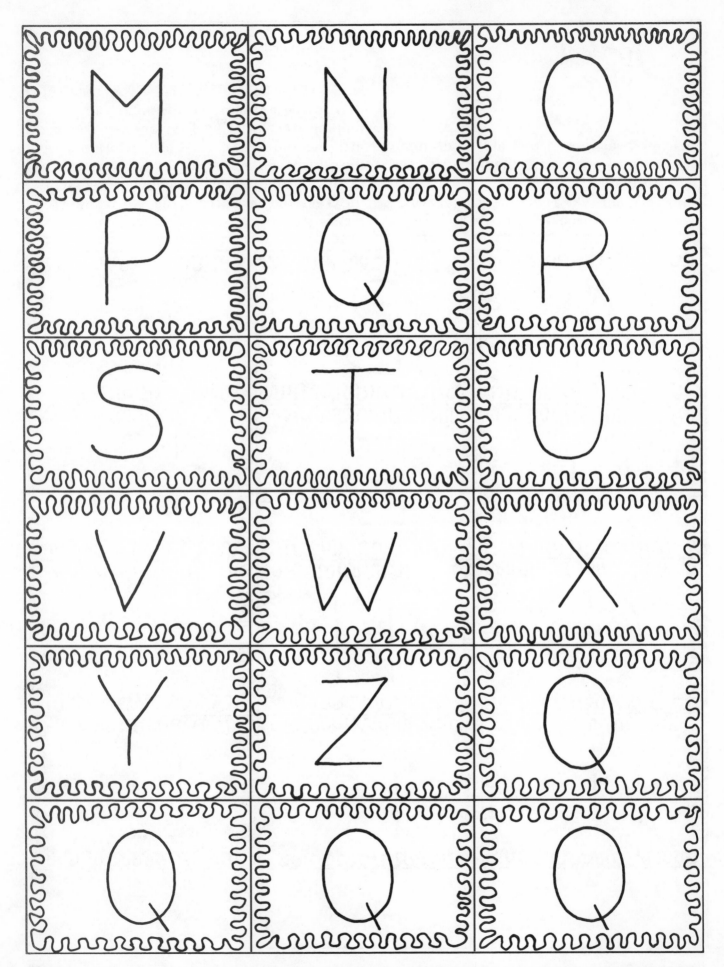

Rr

MOVEMENTS

Rabbits

Tell the children to pretend to be rabbits. Play some lively music to accompany hopping movement. Have a rabbit race and let children hop to a goal line. Tell the children to remember to hold up their ears as they hop!

Ropes

Ask two children to hold the ends of a long rope. Tell them to swing it back and forth. Choose someone to face the rope. As the rope swings toward him or her, the child jumps over it, with feet together. Ask the child to turn around and jump back. When the children can do this, let them jump back and forth continuously facing one of the rope holders. Enlist the help of some older children to help swing the ropes if your children have trouble with this.

Rock 'n' Roll

Tell the children a little bit about the term *rock 'n' roll.* Play some different rock 'n' roll records for the children. Let them move about the way the music makes them feel. Divide the class into groups and have them perform for each other.

Raking Leaves

Let the children pretend to rake leaves in a yard. Tell them to rake with both long and short strokes. They can rake fast and slow to create big and small piles. Ask the entire class to pretend to rake their smaller piles into a giant pile in the center of the play area. If you have thick mats on the play area, the children can pretend to jump on the leaves! Tell them to make the sound of the letter **R** as they rake.

GAMES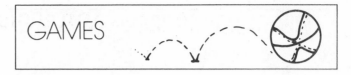

Roll the Ball

Assign the children partners for this activity. Tell the partners to face each other and stand a designated distance away. Give each pair a ball. The object is for one partner to roll the ball through the other partner's legs. The players try not to let it get through, but they must keep their feet in place until the ball passes. A child who succeeds in getting the ball through his or her partner's legs scores a point.

Ringer

Fill some tall thin plastic bottles with sand and cap them. Place them around the play area. Give the children rings, such as canning rings, to toss around the bottles. Let them each keep score on a piece of paper.

Running and Relays

Give the children many opportunities to run. Plan some running just for fun as well as for some individual and relay races. Try some new variations on running such as running backward, sideways, to the left, to the right, in small circles, and in place.

Run, Rabbit, Run

Divide the children into two groups—rabbits and foxes. Choose someone to be the leader of the rabbits, and another child to be the leader of the foxes. Tell the rabbits to stand in a marked circle, which is their safe home. The foxes stand in another area of the playground or gym. Ask the rabbits to go very quietly for a walk to look for food. When the leader of the foxes calls "Run, rabbits, run!" the rabbits hurry back to their safe area. If a rabbit is tagged by a fox, he or she becomes a fox.

Ring Around the Rocket Ship

Ask the children to form a circle with hands joined. Tell the children to slide around the circle to the right while reciting this jingle. At the word "Catch!" everyone drops hands and reaches up. At the word "Fall!" everyone falls down into a ball on the floor. Repeat the jingle, sliding to the left.

> Ring around the rocket ship.
> Try to catch a star.
> Stardust, stardust,
> Fall where you are. (tune of "Ring Around the Rosy")

Red Lion

Mark two goal lines at some distance apart on the play area. Ask the children to stand behind one of the lines. Choose someone to be the red lion, who stands facing the other children in a "den" behind the opposite line. Tell the children to walk up to the red lion, chanting:

Red lion, red lion, come out of your den.
Those whom you catch will be your new friends.

As the children gather around the red lion, call "Come out!" On this signal, the children race back to the starting line. The red lion tries to tag them. Those who are caught become the red lion's helpers. The child who is the last to be caught is the red lion for the next game.

ALPHABET SNACK

Rice and Raisin Faces

Let the children look at and feel some raw brown rice. Cook a batch of the rice for eating according to package directions. When the rice is cooked, give the children some raisins to make faces in their servings of rice. Ask them to form the letter **R** with raisins too. If desired, sprinkle a little cinnamon in the water while cooking.

Other taste experiences for letter **R**: radishes, raspberries, rhubarb, ricotta cheese, rutabagas, and rye bread.

SONGS AND POEMS

Song: "Ring Around the Rainbow"

(tune of "Ring Around the Rosy")

Ring around the rainbow (for ring, *make round shape with hands; for* rainbow, *make hand motion like rainbow*)
Rockets full of **R** (for rockets, *hold hands together above head*)
R-r-r-r. (*sound of* **R**)
The sky is very far. (*hold hand at eyebrows, looking far away*)

Sing this song slowly at first; repeat it several times, speeding up the tempo until you are singing it very quickly.

Poem: "Row, Row, Row Your Raft"

Row, row, row your raft as quickly as you can. (*pretend to row*)
Row, row, row your raft.
Row, row, row your raft as slowly as you can.
Row, row, row your raft.
Roll, roll, roll your hands as quickly as you can. (*roll hands around each other*)
Roll, roll, roll your hands.
Roll, roll, roll your hands as slowly as you can.
Roll, roll, roll your hands.

Poem: "Right and Left"

This is my right hand, I'll raise it up high. (*raise right hand*)
This is my left hand, I'll touch the sky. (*raise left hand*)
Right hand, left hand, roll them around. (*roll hands*)
Left hand, right hand, pound, pound, pound. (*pound one fisted hand on the other*)

RACE CAR RALLY

Teacher Directions: Cut out the gameboard. Color each car a different color. The cars will be used as game markers. Cut out the hexagon and stick a pencil through the center to use as a spinner. This game can be used in three ways:

naming letters, sounds, or words that begin with that letter or sound.

Student Directions: Choose a car and a lane to race in. Put your car on that lane number. Spin the spinner and do as it tells you. Read the words that are right side up. Say the name of the letter your car lands on. If you do not know it, stay where you are and try moving ahead on your next turn. Finish the race. Then, change lanes and play again!

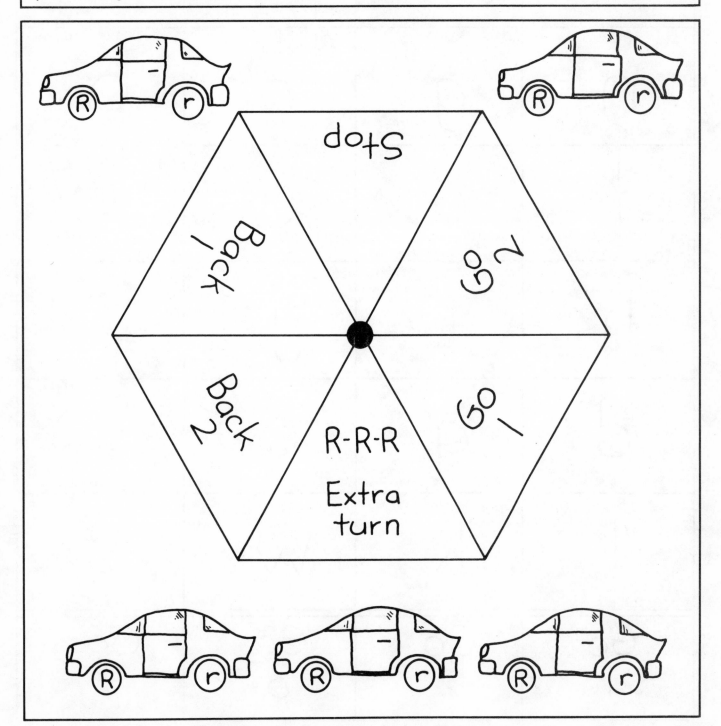

Stop	Stop	Stop	Stop
c	s	m	b
n	g	r	o
t	a	u	f
h	i	j	p
d	q	e	y
l	k	w	z
Go 1	Go 2	Go 3	Go 4

Ss

Silly Spiders

Show the children a picture of a spider or a real one, if possible. Let them count the spider's legs. Let each child choose partners and get down on hands and feet with the partner to form an eight-legged spider. Ask them to try to stay together and crawl around forward and backward and pretend to spin a web.

Seal Walk

Tell the children to lie flat on their stomachs on the floor of the play area. Ask them to push up the upper portion of their bodies and hold themselves up with their arms, which must be straight and stiff at the elbows. Tell the children to "walk" using their hands and dragging their feet and legs behind them.

Snow Fun

Tell the children to pretend that there was just a big snowstorm. Dramatize dressing up to go out to play. Pretend to roll snowballs; have a snowball fight; make a snowman; and make angels-in-the-snow, and then get up to shake off the snow. To end this activity, they might pretend to take off coats, hats, mittens, and boots and to come in for hot chocolate.

Snakes

Let the children pretend to be snakes. Play some music as they slither along the floor. Tell them to make the sound of letter **S** as they move. Give a jump rope to each group of three children. Ask two to hold the ends and to shake the rope on the floor in snaking motions. The other child tries to jump over the snake without touching the rope. Give each child a turn to jump over the snake.

Seesaws

Tell the children you are going to make a big seesaw. Stand facing your group of children. Ask one child to come and stand opposite you and pretend to hold onto the handles on a seesaw. Tell the child to watch you carefully. When you go down, the child must stay up. When you are up, the child must squat down. Then let the children play seesaw with each other, in pairs.

Super Sit-Ups

Ask the children to lie on the floor on their stomachs. Tell them to place their hands on the floor as they would for push-ups. Instead, they roll themselves over and pull themselves up into a sitting position. Make sure the children do this exercise rolling from both the right and left sides.

Sock Hop

Let the children take off their shoes to dance and move in their stocking feet. Play some rousing '50s music to accompany movement. Ask them to try to dance in **S** motions.

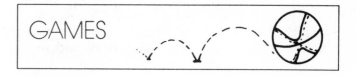

Spoon Ball

Divide the children into small groups for this relay. Give each team a spoon and a small ball such as a Ping-Pong ball. Tell them that each player must race to a designated line and back without dropping the ball. If a racer does drop the ball, he or she must stop, get it, and put it back on the spoon. The first team to finish wins the race. When the activity is over, ask children to put the spoons end-to-end in the shape of the letter **S**.

Simon Says

Teach the children how to play Simon Says. Tell the children that you will give them a direction. They should only perform the action if you precede your statement by saying "Simon Says." Make some of your directions silly. If a child performs the action when you have not said "Simon Says," that child is out. See who plays the longest.

Squirrel and the Nut

Ask the children to stand in a circle holding their hands behind them like little cups. Choose one child to be the silly squirrel. Give the silly squirrel a nut or cork representing a nut. The silly squirrel scampers around the circle and puts the nut into someone's hands. That child chases the silly squirrel, tries to tag him or her before the squirrel reaches the open place, then takes a turn as the silly squirrel. Play until everyone has had a turn to be the silly squirrel.

ALPHABET SNACK

Snake Snacks with Sesame Seeds

Let the children help you measure and mix the following ingredients:

    2 cups whole wheat flour
    1 cup water
    ⅔ cup sesame seeds
    ½ teaspoon baking powder
    3 tablespoons melted butter or margarine

Give each child a little ball of dough to knead. If it gets sticky, provide a little flour to roll it in. Show how to make a snake in the shape of the letter **S** from the dough, then press it flat. Carefully put the snakes into an electric skillet with a little oil and cook both sides until light brown and crispy.

Other taste experiences for letter **S**: salad, salmon, soup, soybeans, spaghetti, spinach, squash, and strawberries.

SONGS AND POEMS

Song: "Something Silly in My Sock"

(tune of "Old MacDonald")

Something silly in my sock *(point to sock)*,
Standing in the sun.
Swinging *(swing body to and fro)*, singing in my sock,
Spiders in my sock. *(make crawling motion with
    fingers)*
With a "s-s" *(sound of* **S***; bend knees)* here and a "s-s"
    there,
Here a "s", there a "s," everywhere a "s-s."
Something silly in my sock, spiders in my sock.

Other verses: Substitute *stick* and *stone* for *sock*.

Poem: "Scarecrow"

Scarecrow, scarecrow, turn around.
Scarecrow, scarecrow, jump up and down.
Scarecrow, scarecrow, arms up high.
Scarecrow, scarecrow, wink one eye.
Scarecrow, scarecrow, bend your knee.
Scarecrow, scarecrow, flop in the breeze.
Scarecrow, scarecrow, climb into bed.
Scarecrow, scarecrow, rest your head.
(imitate motions of scarecrows)

SPIDERWEBS

Teacher Directions: Duplicate a spider card for each player and color the spiders. Cut 15 pieces of string for each web. Cut out the circle. Insert a brass fastener through a paper clip into the center of the circle to make a spinner.

Student Directions: Choose a spider card. Make a web for your spider by putting 15 strings on it. Take turns spinning the spinner. Take off the number of strings the spinner shows. If you spin an **S**, you get an extra turn. Try to get your spider out of the web. You can play this game another way too: Each time you spin, put that many parts on the web. When you have 15, you win!

Tt

MOVEMENTS

Tightropes

Bring a jump rope for each child to the gym or play area. Lay these out in the shape of giant **T**s. Ask the children to pretend the **T**s are tightropes and to walk on them using a heel-to-toe step. Let them try walking backward along the lines. Ask them to try hopping back and forth over the lines of the **T**.

Toe-Touches

Teach the children to do toe-touches. Tell the children to stand up straight and tall with legs together. With hands raised in the air, the children should then bend over slowly and touch their toes. Do this to a count. Next, ask the children to stand with legs apart. Show them how to do crossover toe-touches. Touch the right toe with the left hand and then the left toe with the right hand. Ask the children to sit down on the floor with their legs spread apart. Tell them to stretch their bodies over the right leg and toe and then over the left leg and toe. Tell them to bend over and touch the right hand to right toe and then left hand to left toe at the same time.

Tunnels

Let the children take turns making tunnels by putting their hands and feet on the floor and arching their bodies. Ask them to work in pairs or threes crawling through each other's tunnels. Play a tunnel game. Ask all the children to form a line. The first child in the line forms a tunnel. The children in the line crawl through. When they have gotten through, the new first child in line makes a tunnel. The game is over when everyone has been a tunnel. Divide your class into smaller groups if you would like the tunnels to be smaller.

Turtle Trail

Ask the children to pretend to be turtles crawling on the ground. Give them something to carry on their backs for a shell such as a block, a beanbag, or a small toy. Lay out a trail of cut-out **T**s on the floor for them to crawl beside. Tell them to make the sound of **T** as they crawl past the special letter.

Toss the Ball

Divide the class into several small groups. Ask each group to form a circle. Let them practice tossing the ball to one another. Vary this by asking them to bounce, roll, and kick the ball around the circle. Give each group a tire. Ask them to toss the ball into the tire.

Toy Center

Let the children each choose a toy from home to bring to the group to share. Provide time for the children to play in small groups in this center. Encourage the children to be careful handling each other's toys. Ask them to show you how individual toys move or operate.

GAMES
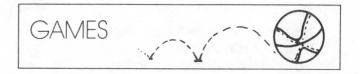

Tiger Tail

Ask the children to form a column. Give a handkerchief to the last child to tuck into the belt or garment waist area. The children in the line form the tiger. The first person in the line tries to steal the tiger's tail by maneuvering the line around. After the tail is taken, the first child in the line goes to the rear to wear the tiger's tail and the game continues. If your group is large, divide it in half or thirds to play this game.

Tambourine Game

Ask the children to form a circle facing in. Let them take turns coming to the center of the circle and shaking a tambourine, calling "**T** is for tambourine!" When a child finishes a turn, he or she taps someone to take a turn. Ask the children to sit down when they have had a turn. When everyone has finished, they can sing a favorite song, while you or one of the children shakes the tambourine to the beat.

Treasure Hunt

Conduct the treasure hunt indoors or outside. Let the children hunt for a treasure item beginning with the letter **T** (tangerines, toys, tops, trucks, etc.). Make a separate clue for each child, and hide the clues. Each clue should have a child's name and a picture of the place where the next clue can be found. When a child finds the clue that he or she is looking for, the new clue is passed on to the child whose name is printed on it. The last clue will have a drawing of the hidden **T** object. Each child helps the group get closer to finding the treasure!

ALPHABET SNACK

Tasty Tuna and Tomato Turtles

Provide a small half or quarter of a tomato for each child's turtle shell. Scoop out the center of each tomato with a spoon. Let them eat the pulp. Ask each child to measure and mix:

> 1 heaping tablespoon tuna, drained
> 1 teaspoon mayonnaise
> A dash of salt and pepper, if desired

Have them plop the tuna mixture onto a plate and press the shell on top of it, forming the body and shell of a turtle. Give each child two small sticks of celery for them to form the letter **T** on the shell of their turtle. (Note: You may have to change the proportions of tuna and mayonnaise depending on the size of your tomatoes. Halved cherry tomatoes work well, too.)

Other taste experiences for letter **T**: tangerines, toast, tomato juice, turkey, turnips.

SONGS AND POEMS

Song: "I'm the Letter *T*"

(tune of "I'm a Little Teapot")

I'm the letter **T**, terrific and tall.
Here is my top. Here are my toes. *(point to head; reach for toes)*

And when I get tongue-tied, I can't talk;
T-t-t-t-t-t-t *(sound of **T**) (on the sound of **T** have children hold their arms straight out from their sides, to form the letter **T**)*

Poem: "Tippy Toe"

Tippy tippy tiptoe, here we go.
Tippy tippy tiptoe, to and fro.
Tippy tippy tiptoe, through the house.
Tippy tippy tiptoe, quiet as a mouse. *(have children tiptoe around the room during this poem)*

TURTLE TRAIL

Teacher Directions: Duplicate these pages for each player. Color and cut out the turtles and put them in a container for each player. Put the alphabet key into the container, too, for reference.

Student Directions: Try to put the turtles in a trail in alphabetical order. Look at the alphabet card to check your lineup. When you have finished, say your ABCs!

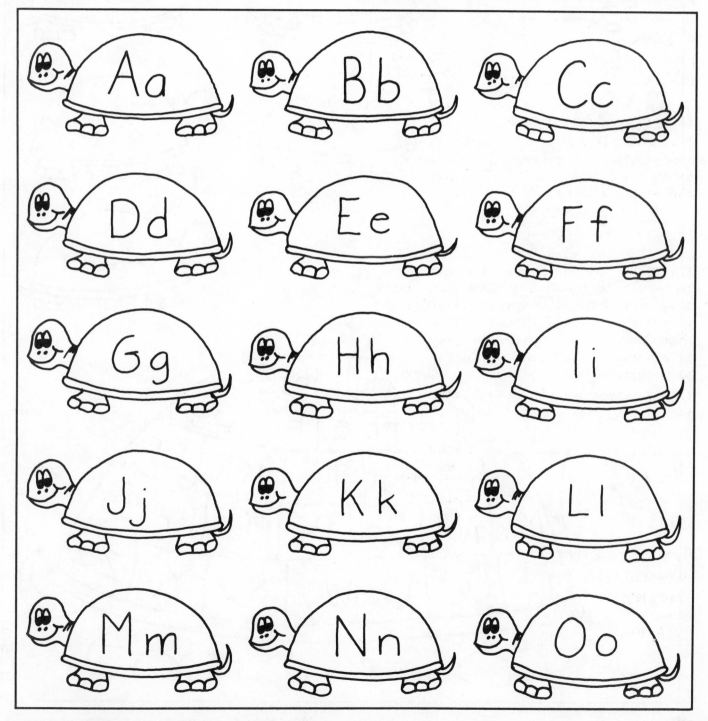

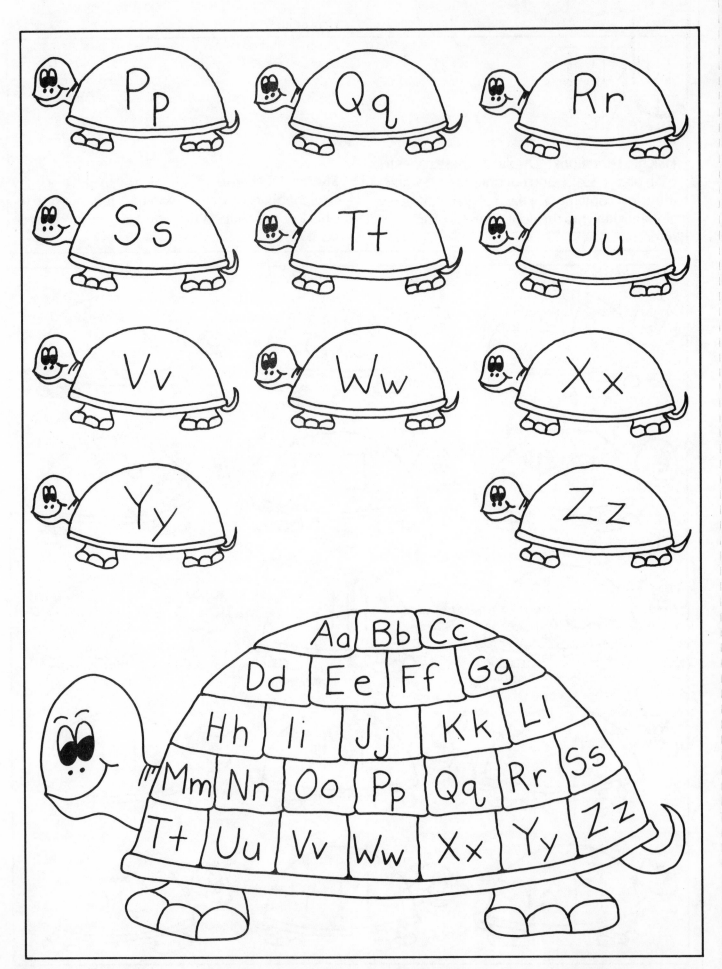

Alphabet Fun and Games reproducible page, copyright © 1984 Pitman Learning, Inc.

Umbrella Day

Ask the children to pretend they are outside for a walk or playing on the playground. Let them creatively move and talk about what they are doing. Then tell them to imagine that they are caught in a rainstorm. Ask them to act out their next movements with their pretend umbrellas.

MOVEMENTS

GAMES

Up, Up, and Away

Give each child an inflated balloon. Tell the children to bat their balloons up. When the balloons come down, the children must catch them before they fall to the floor. If a child's balloon touches the floor, he or she must hold it and sit down. Play several rounds of this game. After this game, divide the children into pairs and ask them to bat the balloons to each other, trying to keep them up, up, up.

Unicorns

Let the children pretend to be unicorns, crawling around on their hands and feet. Ask them to imagine that they have horns in their foreheads. Let them act like horses, tossing their heads from side to side and stretching their necks up high. Ask all the unicorns to prance together and form the letter U on the play area.

U From a Rope

Demonstrate to the children that when a person jumps rope, he or she holds the rope in the shape of the letter U. Ask the children to hold ropes in front of themselves in the shape of the letter U, call "U!" and then jump over the ropes. If children are ready, have them hold the ropes in back of themselves and swing the ropes overhead to jump.

Upper-Body Movements

Ask the children to identify the upper part of their bodies. Ask them to name all the body parts that can move on the upper portion. Play some music and ask the children to move using only their upper torso and its parts. Contrast this experience by using only the bottom part of the body for some movements.

Ugg-a-bugga

Mark two large circles on the floor of the play area at opposite ends of the room. These are the caves of two ugly creatures, the ugg-a-buggas. Choose one child to be an ugg-a-bugga for each cave. Ask those children to sit in the middle of the circles. Let the other children form a ring around the room. Ask them to walk around the room as you play music. Tell them they must step in a cave when they come to one. When the music stops, the ugg-a-buggas tag the child stepping in their circle. They must tag from the sitting position. Whoever is tagged becomes the next ugg-a-bugga.

Up for Seven-Up

This is an indoor game for the group to play. Seat the children in an informal arrangement at tables. Ask them to put their heads down while you go around and tap seven children. Those seven children leave the room. When everyone puts their heads up, the seven children quickly walk into, around, then out of the room. The seated children try to remember the order of the children after they have left the room. Choose seven more children to go out after this round. If seven children at a time is too many for your class, make it a game of Four-Up or Five-Up.

Under-the-Hat Relay

Give each child a stick of some kind—a long twig, a tinkertoy, or a ruler. Divide the children into teams for this relay. Provide a hat for each team. Ask the children to pass the hat among their teammates by using only the sticks to move it along. The first team to pass the hat down the line and back up to the starting person wins.

Under the Umbrella

Choose one child to leave the room, then pick another to hide under an umbrella. (An old blanket or sheet can be used as an umbrella.) Teach the children to sing their inquiry and their responses to the tune of "Are You Sleeping?"

> Who is missing? Who is missing?
> Do you know? Do you know?

The child who left the room sings:

> Is it _____ (child's name)?
> Is it _____ ?

The children respond in one of these ways:

> You are right. You are right.   or
> Guess again. Guess again.

Play until everyone has had a turn to hide under the umbrella.

ALPHABET SNACK

Umbrellas

Thinly slice large round turnips. Give one slice to each child, after cutting a small hole out of the center. Have the children spread one side of the turnip with peanut butter. Let them help wash, peel, and cut carrot sticks for umbrella handles. Give them small chopped pieces of carrots for forming the letter **U** on top of the peanut-buttered turnip. Ask them to stick a carrot stick into the hole in the turnip. They can hold up the umbrella as they eat it! Variation: Cream cheese can be used instead of peanut butter.

Other taste experiences for letter **U**: upside-down cake and unsweetened juices.

SONGS AND POEMS

Song: "Oh, Do You Know the Letter *U*?"

(tune of "Muffin Man")

Oh, do you know the letter **U**, the letter **U**, the letter **U**?
Oh, do you know the letter **U** that makes a sound like this: "ŭ" (*sound of short* **U**)? (*march in a circle as you sing*)

U is for under, under, under. **U** is for under, under we can go.

(*make an arch with hands over your heads; then squat under*)

U is for umbrella, umbrella, umbrella.
U is for umbrella, which we can hold so high.
(*pretend to hold an umbrella*)
U is for ugly, ugly, ugly.
U is for ugly, we can make an ugly face.
(*make scary faces*)

Poem: "Up and Down and Over"

A butterfly came dancing by, up and down and over.
Up and down, up and down, up and down and over.
A honeybee came dancing by, up and down and over.
Up and down, up and down, up and down and over.
A honeybee and butterfly, up and down and over.
Up and down, up and down, up and down and over.
Danced and danced as they flew by, then rested in the clover.
(*use one hand for the butterfly motions and the other for the honeybee motions*)

Poem: "Up and Down"

Up and down, up and down. (*move body up and down*)
Let's pop up. (*act out actions*)
Let's drop down.
Drop down with a bump.
Come up with a jump.
Up, down, up, down, UP! (*jump up high*)

Poem: Ugly Exercise

Uglies, Uglies	Uglies, Uglies
Fly to the tree.	Crawl to find a sink.
Uglies, Uglies,	Uglies, Uglies
Fly back to me.	Pretend to take a drink.
Uglies, Uglies,	Uglies, Uglies
Gallop to the wall.	Stretch up high.
Uglies, Uglies	Uglies, Uglies
Skip back one and all.	Try to reach the sky.
Uglies, Uglies	Uglies, Uglies
Go and touch a door.	Crawl just like a worm.
Uglies, Uglies	Uglies, Uglies
Lay down on the floor.	Squirm, squirm, squirm!

Actions: Ask the children to be the "Uglies." As you say the poem, ask the Uglies to make the motions.

UNLUCKY **U**

Teacher Directions: Cut apart and color the cards. Cover one side with clear contact paper (optional). Make a simple card holder for each player by duplicating two circles on heavy paper and fastening them in the center with a brass fastener. The children can put their cards between the two circles.

Student Directions: Take a card holder. Pass out all of the cards. Arrange your cards in your holder. If you have a matching pair, lay them down. Take turns drawing a card from another player, trying to make pairs. Lay your pairs down. The person left with the "**U**" is the unlucky one! This game is just like "Old Maid."

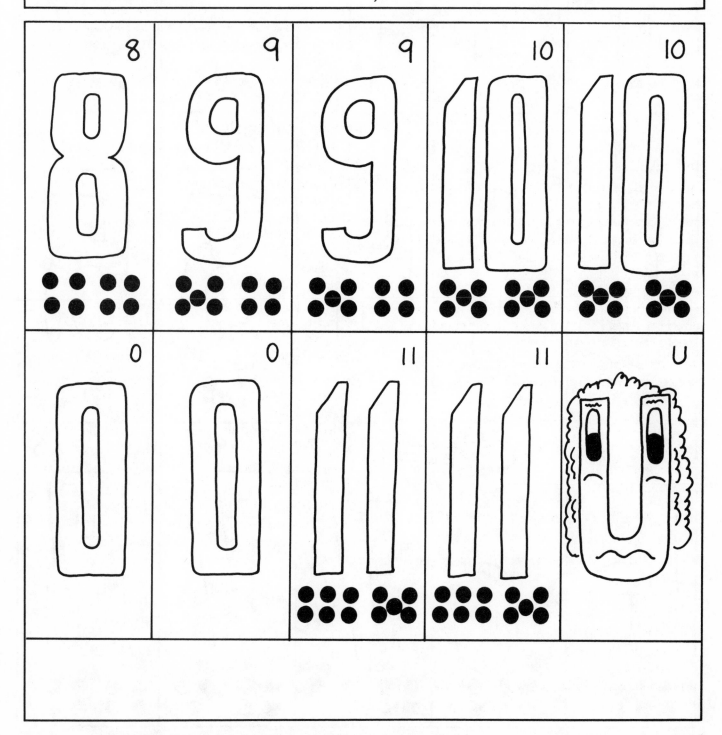

MOVEMENTS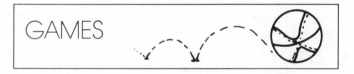

Vampires

Tell the children to pretend they are vampires. Play some spooky music and tell them to make some movements they think vampires would make. Ask them to greet other vampires with the sound of **V** and by making a **V** with their fingers.

Vampires on Vacation

Let the children pretend to be "vampires on vacation." This should be a special "exercise" vacation. Tell the children to do these exercises spookily as a vampire might: jumping jacks, sit-ups, jumps, bicycles, and toe-touches. Ask the children to think of ways to form **V**s with their bodies as they exercise. After they exercise, ask them to lie down in pairs forming the letter **V** and to make the sound of that letter.

V-Jumps

Ask the children to crouch down as low as possible. When you call **V**, they should jump up as high as they can, forming a letter **V** with their arms.

GAMES

Vegetable Soup

Ask the children to sit in a circle. They may sit on carpet squares or in chairs. Assign a vegetable to each child, assigning each vegetable twice. Choose one child to start the game. That child goes to the center of the circle and calls out the name of a vegetable. The two children assigned with that vegetable's name must exchange places before the child in the center steals one of their places. If the child in the center is success-

ful in finding a place, he or she takes the name of the vegetable from the displaced child. The child who calls vegetable names in the center can also call "Vegetable Soup!" Then everyone must find a new place. To make this game more concrete, give the children cards that have drawings of their vegetable.

Vanishing Valentine

Ask the children to form a circle. Choose one child to be blindfolded to sit in the middle of the circle. Tape a valentine to a bell. Place the bell under the chair of the blindfolded child. Choose another child to quietly come up, steal the bell, and return to the circle with the bell. Tell everyone in the circle to put their hands behind their backs as if they were each ringing a bell. The child in the center takes off the blindfold and tries to guess who has the bell by listening where the sound is coming from. Play until everyone has had a turn to be blindfolded.

Vase Game

Divide the children into teams. Provide a container (serving as a vase) for each team. Let the children take turns dropping spring clothespins into the vase. They can kneel on a chair and drop the clothespins over the back of the chair into the vase. Let each child have a turn to drop three. Keep track of the points for each team. Ask the children if they can find the shape of letter **V** in the clothespin. Lay all the clothespins end-to-end on the floor in the shape of letter **V** when the game is finished.

V Ball

Tape the letter **V** to a large ball for this game. Stand in the center of the circle, throw the ball in the air, and call one of the children's names. The child must come and catch the ball before it bounces, calling "**V**!" Simplify this game by letting the ball bounce one or two times.

Vampires in Vans

Divide the children into three groups. Group A children are van fronts; Group B children are van backs; and Group C children are vampires. Tell each child from Group A to find a partner from Group B to form a van (like a bridge), arching their arms overhead and clasping each other's hands. The vans should each find an area on the playground or in the gym to "park" that is not too close to another van. Each child from the vampire group finds a van to stand in. Explain to the children that each time you blow the whistle, each vampire must run to find a new van. Tell them that they cannot go to the same van two times in a row.

Exchange the jobs for each group so that each child has the opportunity to do all three things.

ALPHABET SNACK

Vanishing Variety

Explain to the children what the word "variety" means. Tell them they will make a snack using a variety of foods. Let children create their own variety by putting spoonfuls of each of these things into small cups and stirring them up:

> Dried fruit bits (apricots, apples, dates, figs, etc.)
> Coconut
> Peanuts
> Sunflower seeds
> Raisins
> Walnuts, broken in small pieces

Tell the children to make their variety snacks vanish. Ask them to write imaginary **V**s in the air before they take bites of their snack.

Other taste experiences for letter **V**: vegetables and vanilla pudding.

SONGS AND POEMS

Song: "The Village Game"

(tune of "In and Out the Window")

Go round and round the village, the village, the village. Go round and round the village, as we have done before. *(children walk around in a circle singing)*

Go in and out the village, the village, the village. Go in and out the village, as we have done before. *(choose one child to weave in and out of the children as they raise their joined hands in arches)*

We all can make a **V**, a **V**, a **V**. We all can make a **V**, as we have done before. *(children hold hands above heads in shape of **V** as they sing)*

Song: "Where, Oh Where, is Letter *V*?"

(tune of "Where, Oh Where, Is My Friend?")

Where, oh where, is letter **V**? *(for where, hold hands at sides as if questioning; for **V**, form **V** with fingers)*

Where, oh where, is letter **V**?
Where, oh where, is letter **V**?
V is under the veil, v-v *(sound of* **V***). (for veil, hold hands over face)*

Other verses: Substitute *vest, vegetables,* and *volcano* for *veil.*

Actions: For *vest,* point to shirt; for *vegetables,* pretend to pull them out of ground; for *volcano,* hold arms over head touching hands.

Poem: "Five Little Vampires"

Five little vampires sitting on the floor, *(hold up five fingers)*
One jumped up, and then there were four. *(close fist and "jump" with thumb)*
Four little vampires as still as can be, *(hold up four fingers)*
One sat on a chair, and then there were three. *(hold pointed index finger as if it were sitting on other hand)*
Three little vampires looking right at you, *(hold up three fingers)*
One crawled away, and then there were two. *(make crawling motion with third finger on desk or table)*
Two little vampires sitting having fun, *(hold up two fingers)*
One flew like a bird, and then there was one. *(make fourth finger flutter up and down)*
One little vampire left all alone, *(hold up little finger)*
Decided to leave, so then there were none. *(curl last finger into fist)*

Poem: "Verses"

Teach the children to jump rope (or jump in place) to the rhythm of these verses.

Bubble gum, bubble gum,
Chew and blow.
Bubble gum, bubble gum,
Scrape your toe.
Bubble gum, bubble gum,
Tastes so sweet.
Get that bubble gum
Off your feet!

Ice cream soda, Delaware punch,
Tell me the name of your honey bunch.
Alphabet A, B, C, D, . . . *(and so on until the child misses or completes the alphabet)*

Lady, lady, at the gate.
Eating cherries from a plate.
How many cherries can she eat?
One, two, three, four, . . . *(and so on)*

SPOT THE VAMPIRE

Teacher Directions: Duplicate one vampire and one set of spots for each small group of players. Color the vampire and his spots.

Student Directions: Cover each letter with a spot so that the letters do not show. Take turns uncovering the letters. If you can name the letter, you keep the spot. Try to get lots of spots!

Variation: Children can name things for each letter or make the sound of the letter.

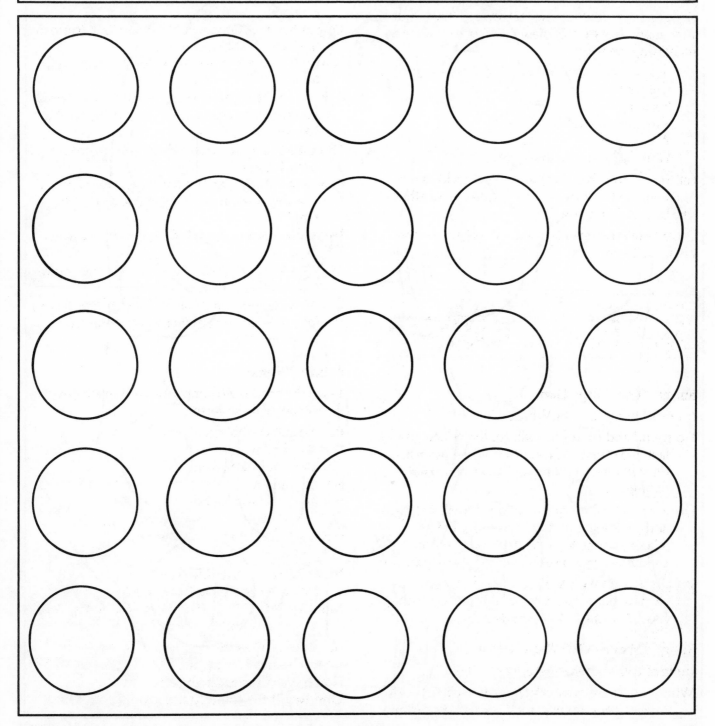

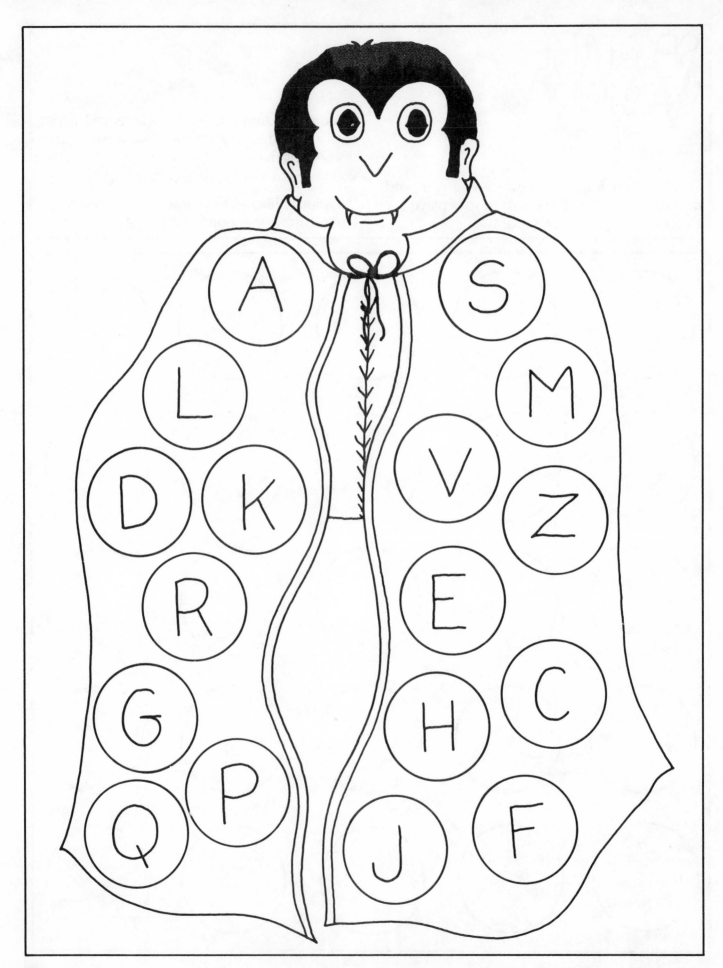

Alphabet Fun and Games reproducible page, copyright © 1984 Pitman Learning, Inc.

Ww

MOVEMENTS

Wind and Waves

Provide some old sheets. Divide the class into small groups and give each group a sheet. Let them stand around the sheet, holding it in their hands. Let them shake it to make waves. Tell them the wind is blowing gently or strong. They should make the waves the correct size. Give each group a Wiffle ball to put on the sheet to toss about on the waves.

Wands

Cut a ¾-inch dowel rod about three feet long for each child. Have the children move their bodies in relation to the wand: move around the wand, jump over it, crawl over and under it, move it to the left and right, hold it in the right and left hands, do stretches with it, roll it with their feet, and hold it between the hands and do toe touches with it. When you have completed this activity, ask everyone to try to form a big **W** with the wands.

Walking Board

Conduct a small group of children using a walking board—a long plank of wood about 6–8 inches wide, placed on the floor. Tape a **W** to the wall and ask the children to focus on it as they try some of these activities: walk forward, sidestep, walk backward, walk carrying a ball, walk on all fours, walk with hands folded on chest, hop along the board.

Weaving

Set up chairs or some other item in a line on the play area with a space between each item. Let the children "weave" through the arrangement using different movements: walking, skipping, running, hopping, galloping, and tiptoeing.

Walking and Clapping

Begin as the leader. Tell the children to either walk or clap. If you clap, the children must walk. If you walk, the children must stop walking and clap as they stand in place. Let different children take your place as the leader of this exercise.

Walking with a Wiggle

Let the children improvise ways to walk with a wiggle. As they walk around, let them wave to each other making the sound of **W**. Encourage them to make their wiggles with different body parts such as the head, nose, hands, arms, legs, feet, or knees. Let each child walk a line showing how to walk with a wiggle. Give everyone a round of applause.

Wiggle Boxes

Ask the children to sit or stand in front of you. Tell them they will be wiggle boxes. They must watch you very closely. When you turn the imaginary knob to "on," they wiggle all over. When they see you turn the knob to "off," they freeze. If they see you press a button, that means they are to make the sound of **W** continuously until you press the button again.

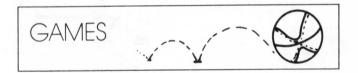

GAMES

Windchase

Teach the children this verse:

> Here I am, Wind. Watch what I can do.
> Try to catch me but I'll get away from you!

Ask the children to stand in a large circle with space between each player. Choose someone to be the wind to stand inside the circle. Choose another child to be a wiggly worm. The worm wiggles and weaves in and out around the children in the circle as they chant the verse. The wind tries to catch the worm at the end of the verse. Give all the children a turn to be either the wind or the worm.

Wheelbarrows

Ask each child to find a partner. Explain how to play the wheelbarrow game. One child is the wheelbarrow, and the other child is the mover of the wheelbarrow. The wheelbarrow gets down on the floor on hands and knees. The mover carefully lifts the legs of the other child and holds them up as the child walks on his or her hands. Hold wheelbarrow relay races.

ALPHABET SNACK

Wonderful Waffle Worms

Let the children help you measure and mix:

    1 cup sifted unbleached flour
    ¾ cup stirred whole wheat flour
    1 teaspoon baking soda
    1 teaspoon baking powder
    ½ teaspoon salt
    2 eggs
    ⅓ cup oil
    2 cups buttermilk

Beat very well until everything is mixed. Pour the batter in worm shapes on the waffle iron when it is hot. Let the children cut up different fruits to put on top of the waffles. With leftover fruit, the children can form the letter **W**.

Other taste experiences for letter **W**: Waldorf salad, walnuts, watermelon, wheat germ, and wax beans.

SONGS AND POEMS

Poem: "Wacky Witch"

The wacky witch stood up. *(stand up and keep body bent as a witch)*

She watched to the right. *(hand above eyes looking to the right)*

She watched to the left. *(hand above eyes looking to the left)*

She watched what was up. *(hand above eyes looking up)*

She watched what was down. *(hand above eyes looking down)*

And then she got on her broom and flew away, WHOOSH! *(pretend to get on broom and fly away)*

Song: "*W-W* Through My Window"

(tune of "Bluebird Bluebird")

W-w through my window.
W-w through my window.
W-w through my window.
Wah, wah, wah, wah, wah, wah, wah. *(for **W**, hold

index and third fingers of both hands in shape of **W**; *for window, form a square with fingers; for wah, wiggle all over)*

Other verses: Substitute *walrus, witchie, worms,* and *water* for **W**.

Actions: For *walrus,* make tusks with hands; for *witchie,* form witch hat over head; for *worms,* point finger and slide it through air; for *water,* pretend to swim.

WINDOW WONDERS

Teacher Directions: Duplicate the "windows" on heavy paper. Tape a small block to each end so that they stand. Provide marbles and counters (unpopped popcorn, dried beans, or buttons) for each player. Cut out a wheel for each player to use as a plate to hold the counters. Put a tape line on the floor 2 to 3 feet from the windows.

Student Directions: Pick your own set of windows or share one with a friend and take turns. Sit behind the tape. Roll a marble and try to get it through a window. If you do get it through a window, take the number of counters the window shows and put them on your wheel. At the end of the playing time, add how many counters you have.

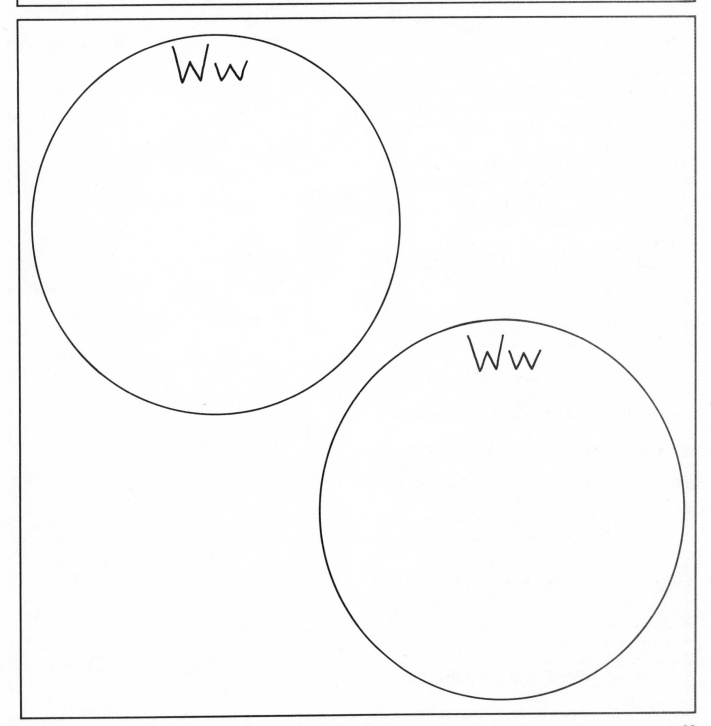

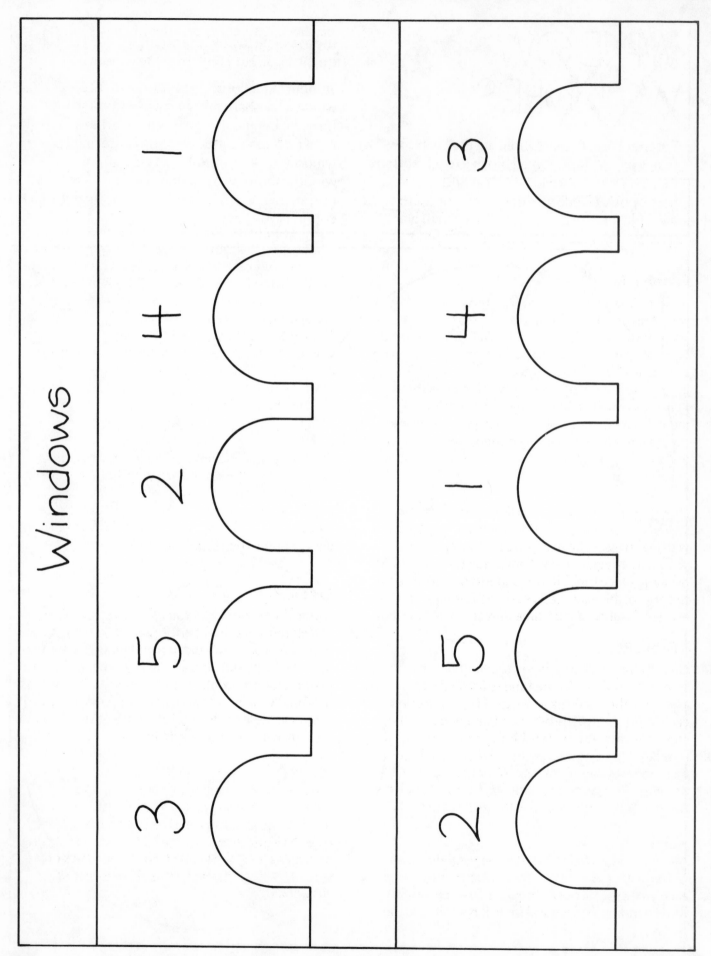

Windows

3 5 2 4 1

2 5 1 4 3

MOVEMENTS

play area. Tell them to make long jumps, short jumps, backward jumps, sideways jumps, tip-toe jumps, and jumps in a circle.

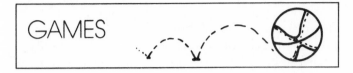

GAMES

Xylophone

Ask the children to stand in one straight line facing you. Walk down the line and as you tap the children, ask them to squat down quickly. Walk back the other direction, tapping and telling the children to stand up again quickly. Tell them to go down again one at a time without your taps, just by watching the person right before them and moving immediately after them. For a variation, ask the children to go up and down from a lying to a sitting position and from a sitting to a lying position.

X-Legs

Show the children how to do this exercise. With feet in stride position, jump up and cross legs in midair. Land with legs crossed. With legs crossed, jump up again and uncross legs in midair, landing again in the stride position. Once the children understand and are able to perform this exercise, speed up the tempo and have everyone call out **X** each time they are in that position.

X Over a Rope

Give each child a jump rope. Ask the children to spread out on the play area and to lay their ropes out in a line. Tell them to walk along their ropes, crossing each leg in front of the other and stepping over the rope sideways slightly. Tell them not to step on their ropes. Ask them to look for the **X** shape their legs make as they cross them over. After this, ask the children to find a partner. Tell them to form an **X** with the two ropes and hop around in the sections of the **X**.

X Jumps

Ask the children to begin this activity standing as a group in the shape of the letter **X**. Tell them to jump each time you call out **X**. They can do some jumps while standing in place and some jumps around the

X-citement!

Ask the children to hold hands and form a circle. Choose two children to go to the center of the circle. Blindfold one of them and give a noisemaker of some kind—such as a can filled with marbles—to the other. Ask the child with the noisemaker to keep shaking the can and moving around the circle as the blindfolded child tries to tag him or her by listening for the sound. Give each child a chance to be the blindfolded child and the noisemaker. The children in the circle prevent anyone from leaving the boundaries of the circle by holding them in. This will prove to be **X**-citing!

X Tag

Divide the class into four groups and put one group in each corner of the play area or gym. Choose someone to be "It." "It" stands in the center and uses both hands and arms crossed in an **X** position to point to two groups to change places. As they run, "It" tries to tag someone. The person tagged becomes the new "It."

Get the X

Divide the children into pairs. Give a rope to each pair of children that will be performing the activity at one time. Have each pair hold its rope tightly. Place a plastic bottle filled with sand about six feet behind each player. Label the bottles with the letter **X**. On your verbal signal **X**, each partner pulls the other to see who can get to the **X** bottle first. Let them try twice, first with the right hands and then with the left.

Hit the X

Tape several sheets of paper marked with **X**s to the walls around the play area. Divide the children into small groups and assign each group to an **X**. Tell the children to practice throwing balls or beanbags at the wall, trying to hit the **X**. Let children keep track of the times they hit the **X** with tally marks on paper or chalkboard.

Steal the *X*

Divide the children into two equal teams. Create pairs of players by assigning the same number to two children, one child on either team. Tape or pin a card on each player with that assigned number. Ask the teams to stand opposite each other on two lines. In the center, place an eraser or a block with an **X** taped to it. When you call out a number, the two children with that number race forward to steal the **X** and take it back to their teams. The child who does not get it may try to tag the other child. If the child is successful, he or she earns a point for that team. If the child who steals the **X** is not caught, he or she earns a point for the team. Call all the numbers several times.

X-in-a-Box Relay

Divide the children into relay teams of equal numbers. Give each child a cut-out paper **X**. Tell them to run to an empty box at the end of their line; drop in the **X**; then run back and tap the next player, calling "**X**!" as they do so. Reverse the race by having the children run to the box and bring back their **X**s.

ALPHABET SNACK

X-tra Good *X*s

Purchase about one pound of fresh green beans. Let the children snap off the ends of the beans. Leave them long. After washing them, cook the beans in about an inch of salted water. Cook uncovered at a boil for five minutes, then cover and boil until tender, about 15 to 25 minutes longer. Serve to the children and ask them to lay the beans out in the shape of the letter **X**.

Other taste experiences for the letter **X**: long, flat, cooked noodles or strips of cheese for forming the letter **X**; extra-good pudding to draw **X**s in before it's gobbled up!

SONGS AND POEMS

Song: "Where Is *X*?"

(tune of "Where Is Thumbkin?")

Where is **X**? Where is **X**?
Here I am. Here I am.
How are you today, **X**?
Very fine, I thank you.
X away. **X** away.

*(Sing the song four times. The first time, form an **X** with the fingers. The second time, form an **X** with the hands. The third time, form an **X** with the arms, and the last time, form it with the whole body. Start the first verse softly and increase the volume each time you sing it.)*

Poem: "Stretching *X*s"

Stretch up high, stretch down low. Raise your arms
    and away we go.
Make a circle in the air, sweep your arms around.
Now the other, do the same, and jump up off the
    ground.
We like to bend our **X**s. We like to stretch them, too.
We make our muscles strong. Bend **X**, stretch **X**, bend
    X, stretch **X**,
All day long.
First I bend my knees, then I stand up tall. Down, up,
    down, up, like a rubber ball.
First I'm short **X**, and then I'm tall.

*(stand with body in the shape of an **X** and perform the motions indicated by the poem)*

PUZZLES

Teacher Directions: Duplicate and color the
X puzzles. Cut them apart and put them into an
envelope or box.

Student Directions: Try to fit the **X** puzzles
together by matching words. Try to read them!

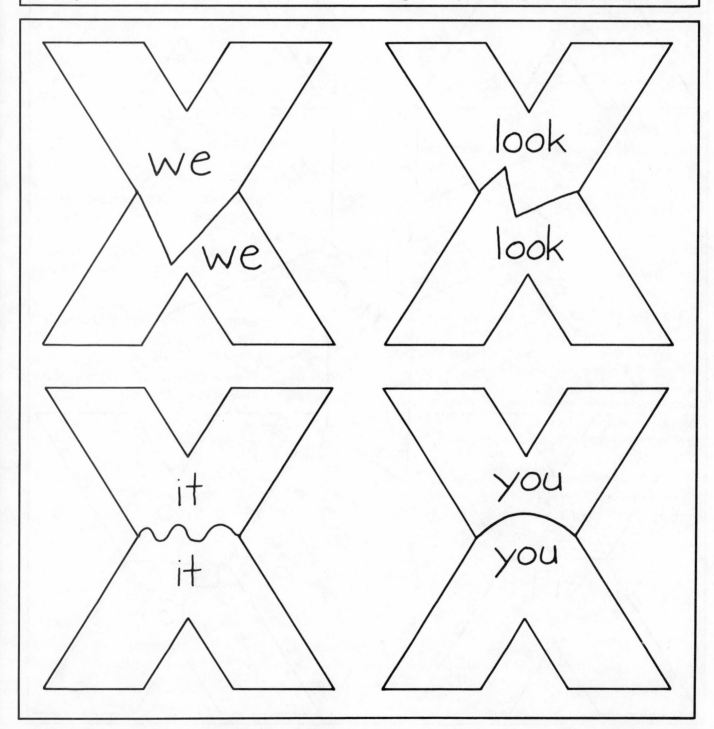

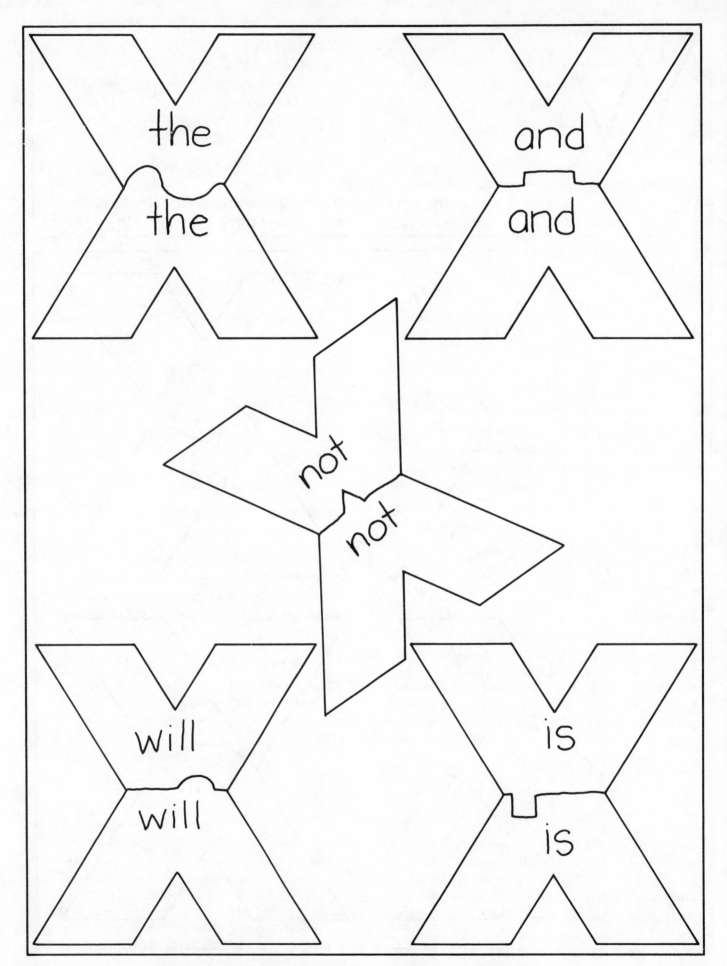

MOVEMENTS

Movement for *Y*

Tell the children to repeat whatever you say and do. Perform these words and actions for them to copy:

Y, Y, I like Y. *(stand in shape of* Y *with arms overhead and legs together)*

Move your **Y**, move your **Y**, very slowly like I. *(on tiptoe, walk slowly holding arms up)*

Jump your **Y**, jump your **Y**, jump your **Y**, jump your **Y**. *(hop around holding arms up)*

Bend your **Y**, bend your **Y**, bend your **Y**, bend your **Y**. *(bend over from the waist and touch hands to the ground)*

Skip your **Y**, skip your **Y**, skip your **Y**, skip your **Y**. *(skip around holding arms up)*

Yes, **Y**. Yes, **Y**. Yes, **Y**. Yes, **Y**. *(stand in place and sway arms from side to side)*

Yakity Yaks

Bring pictures of yaks to show the group. Talk about this animal. Ask the children to get down on hands and feet and pretend to be yaks in a yak yard. Ask them to crawl forward and backward. Tell them to move quickly and very slowly. Play some music to accompany movement. Let them greet each other with the sound of **Y**.

Yards of Yellow Yarn

Give each child a yard of yellow yarn. Ask them to try some of these actions with the yarn: make shapes with it; make the letter **Y**; jump, hop, crawl, and bear-walk over and around it; lay it out in a line and jump back and forth over it; then make letters from it and make an action for each—jump for **J**, hop for **H**, tiptoe for **T**, crawl for **C**, and run for **R**. Direct the children to make some of these movements first to the *left* and then to the *right*.

Yogurt in a Dish

Let the children pretend to be yogurt in a dish. Ask them to stand, sit, and lay on the floor, then to droop like frozen yogurt or to wiggle and jiggle like yogurt in a dish. Let each child tell what flavor of yogurt he or she represents.

GAMES

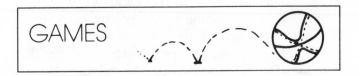

Yak, Yak, Yak, You!

Ask the children to form a circle. This game is a version of "Duck, Duck, Goose." Choose one child to go around the circle and to tap each child and say "Yak, Yak." When the child taps someone and says "You," that person chases the first child around the circle trying to tag him or her before the child reaches the empty spot in the circle. Ask the children to sit down after they have had a turn.

You Who?

Hang an old sheet or blanket in the room. Cut out two small holes for eyes. Pin the word "you" under the holes. Ask one child to leave the room. Choose someone to stand behind the blanket with eyes at the holes. The rest of the group remains where they are. Ask the child out of the room to return and try to identify the person behind the blanket. Let the children make **Y**s to help decorate the blanket. Use the blanket for other things during the week—a stage for a play, a quiet place, etc.

Yanking Tug-of-War

Roll up an old sheet. Divide the children into two teams and let them try to pull the other team over a long **Y** you have taped or marked on the floor. Ropes can also be used. Divide the children into teams of two for this activity after you have played it with the entire group.

The Yo-Yo Game

Ask the children to stand in a line at one end of the play area. Tell them they will be the yo-yo at the end of a string. They must watch your arm as you pull in and throw out and must make their bodies move as if they were being pushed and pulled. Vary the timing of the pushes and pulls, making some very slow and others very fast. Let some of the children take your place as the leader of this activity. Once the children understand this exercise, let them divide into smaller play groups, with one child being the yo-yo puller for each group.

Yea for *Y*!

Divide the children into teams of pairs. Give each team a lid from a jar with the letter **Y** printed on it. Give each team a ball. Place lids on the floor, between each pair. Each child bounces the ball back and forth to the partner, trying to hit the lid on the bounce, moving it toward the partner. The children cannot step out of place. After a designated period of time, call out "**Y**!" to signal the bouncing to stop. The children who successfully moved the lids closer to their partners by the end of the game can all shout "Yeah!"

Yo-Yos

Ask the children to bring yo-yos from home. Let the children practice their yo-yo-ing skills. Have a simple yo-yo contest and invite another group to witness the event. Let all the contestants design a **Y** to wear for the contest.

ALPHABET SNACK

Yamwiches

Scrub and peel some yams for your class. Ask the children to use their imaginations to think of what else the yam looks like. Ask the children to watch as you slice the yams into thin slices. Give each child two yam slices to make a sandwich. They can spread one slice with peanut butter or cream cheese and them form the letter **Y** with raisins or cut-up fruits or vegetables. After putting the top slice over the filling, they can enjoy a new kind of sandwich—a "yamwich!" Variation: prepare mashed yams and allow the children to draw **Y**s in the yams before eating them.

Other taste experiences for **Y**: yellow jello, Yorkshire pudding, yogurt, and yolks of eggs.

SONGS AND POEMS

Song: "We Wish You a Happy *Y* Week!"

(tune of "We Wish You a Merry Christmas")

We wish you a happy **Y** week, we wish you a happy **Y** week, we wish you a happy **Y** week, Y-y-y-y-y. (sound of letter **Y**) *(stand like letter **Y** with hands stretched out above shoulders)*

Let's all yodel now for **Y** week, let's all yodel now for **Y** week, let's all yodel now for **Y** week, Y-y-y-y-y. *(cup hands at mouth and raise head)*

Let's all yell "YEA!" for **Y** week, let's all yell "YEA!" for **Y** week, let's all yell "YEA!" for **Y** week, Y-y-y-y-y. *(shake hands above head)*

Let's yo-yo now for **Y** week, let's yo-yo now for **Y** week, let's yo-yo now for **Y** week, Y-y-y-y-y. *(make arm and hand go up and down as if playing with yo-yo)*

Let's all roll yarn for **Y** week, let's all roll yarn for **Y** week, let's all roll yarn for **Y** week, Y-y-y-y-y. *(make action of rolling yarn)*

Poem: "Yaks"

One, two, three, four, five. *(count fingers)*
Five little yaks standing in a row. *(hold up five fingers)*
This little yak stubbed his toe. *(point to thumb)*
This little yak said, "Oh, oh, oh!" *(point to index finger)*
This little yak laughed and was glad. *(point to third finger)*
This little yak cried and was sad. *(point to fourth finger)*
This little yak was thoughtful and good. *(point to pinky)*
She ran for the doctor as fast as she could. *(stick out pinky and shake hand)*

YAKITY YAK

Teacher Directions: Color the gameboard and cut it out. Color each yogurt marker a different color and cut them out. Cut out the spinner. Punch a hole in the center and stick a pencil through it.

Student Directions: Choose a colored yogurt marker and put it in one of the corners of the gameboard. Take turns spinning the spinner. Move the number of spaces the spinner shows. Try to get to the yak with *your* yogurt first!

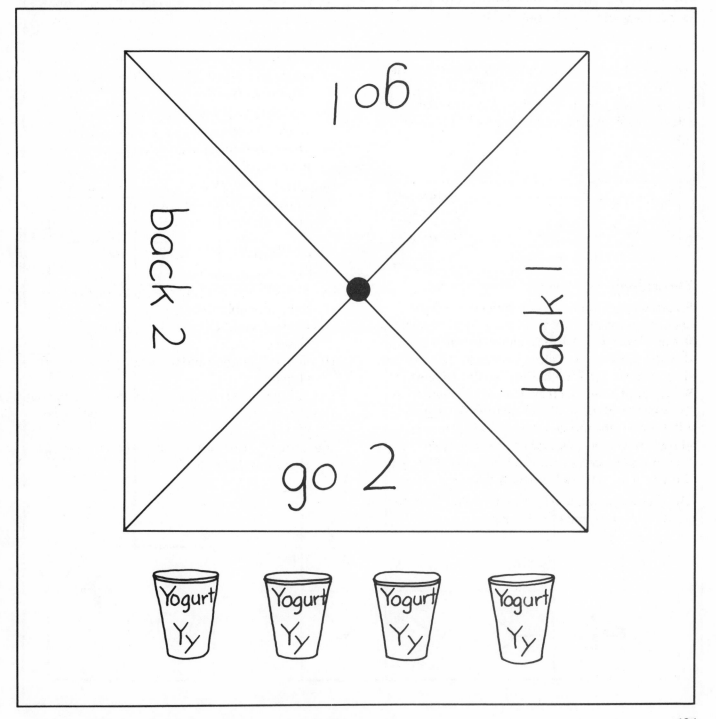

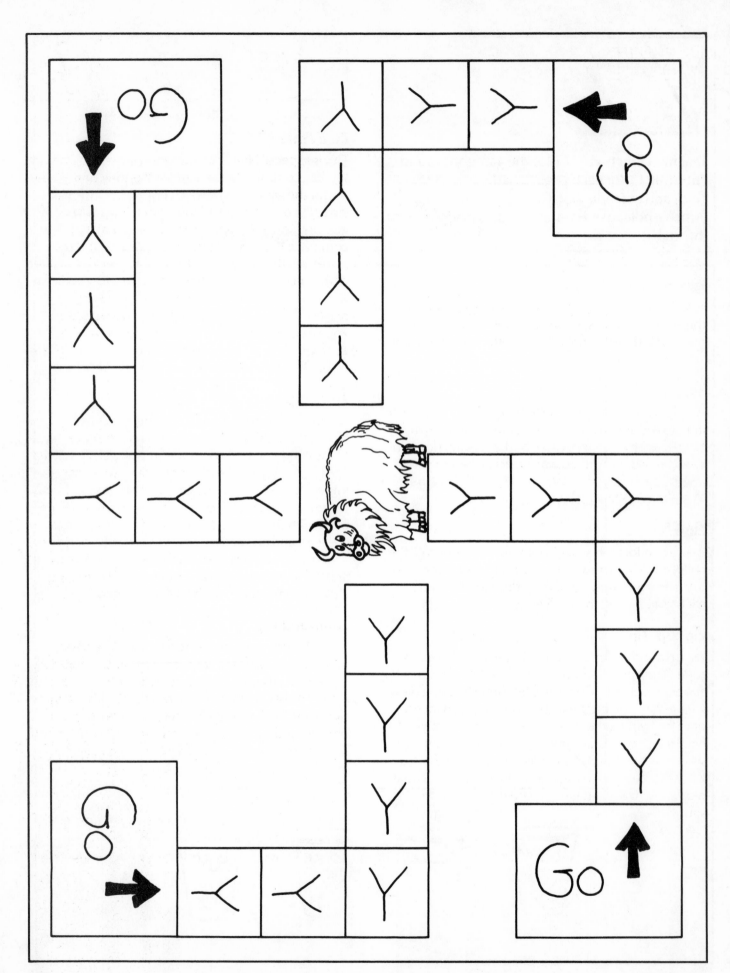

Alphabet Fun and Games reproducible page, copyright © 1984 Pitman Learning, Inc.

Zz

 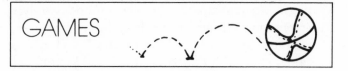
MOVEMENTS

Zebras

Ask the children to pretend to be galloping zebras. Let them move from a standing position to all fours. Tell the zebras to make the sound of letter **Z** as they gallop around.

Zippers

Ask the children to pretend to be zippers. Ask them to imitate you as you move your hands up and down. Have them move their whole bodies up and down in deep knee bends. Play some musical scales or play a record, and let the children stretch up and reach down to the music. Vary the tempo of the scales.

Zip-Ups

Ask the children to work in pairs to do sit-ups. Tell the children to hold down their partner's feet as they take turns doing sit-ups. Ask the children to call "Zip!" each time they lift themselves up.

Zip, Zip, Zip

Assign the children partners. Give each pair a jump rope. Show the children how to hold the ends to swing a rope. Teach them to make a *big* circle by using the whole arm, not just the wrist. Give them a chance to practice twirling the rope. If they are ready, let the children practice jumping rope, with two children swinging the ends. Let them listen for the sound "zip, zip, zip" as the rope swings around. Variation: Rub pieces of corduroy together to make the "zip, zip" sound.

Zero Zone

This is a special kind of tag. Choose one child to be "It." Show all the children where the zone boundaries are for the game. Everyone except "It" should make a circle ("a zero") in the middle of the zone. When "It" gives a command, everyone will scatter and run. The command might be "Zone Zero!" When "It" tags someone, that person must join hands with "It." Either of the two children can then tag players. Anyone who is tagged must join the line and can then tag other players. Anyone who is caught stepping outside the zone must join the line. After everyone is caught, the zone will have zero players left! Choose a new "It" and begin the game again.

Zoo Soup

Ask the children to sit on chairs in a large circle. Choose one child to be the cook. Have the cook come to the center of the circle. Take away the cook's chair. Tell the cook to choose five or six different children as ingredients for the soup, naming each with an animal name as they are tapped to come to the center of the circle with the cook. The cook then says it is time to stir the soup and pretends to stir it with an imaginary stick. When the cook taps the floor three times, the cook and the animals race for an empty seat. The leftover child becomes the cook for the next round.

Zoom and Tug

Tie a 12-foot rope together securely at the ends to form a circle. Let three children at a time get inside the circle, spaced evenly, facing out, and holding the rope at their waists. Let them try to move each other around by pulling on the rope with their waists. Set some objects up about five or six feet from each of them and let them have a contest to see who can maneuver toward and grab the object first.

Follow the Zebra

Ask the children to stand in a large circle with their hands stretched out in front of them, palms up. Choose someone to be a zebra to prance in the center of the circle and to tap someone on the hands gently. The child who is tapped must follow the "zebra" around and do whatever he or she does. They must go around the outside of the circle walking, skipping, hopping, etc. After one round of the circle, the child who followed the zebra becomes the zebra and the game continues.

Zoom Around

Ask the children to form a large circle. Choose one player to be "It" to go to the center of the circle with a ball. Tell the person who is "It" to toss the ball to someone in the circle. The child who catches the ball runs and places the ball in the center of the circle and then chases "It." "It" tries to get back and touch the ball before being tagged by the second player. If "It" is unsuccessful, the second player becomes "It" and the games continues. Place a towel or mat in the center of the circle so the ball will not roll away.

Zip to the Zoo

Tell the children to join hands in a circle. Choose one player to run around outside the circle. Tell that player to stop between two players and call "Zip to the zoo!" Those two players race around the circle in opposite directions. The one who is the first to return to the vacant space is "It" for the next game. Vary this game by asking children to skip or hop around the circle instead of run.

ALPHABET SNACK

Zooloos

Divide the children into groups of three. Let them scrub carrots and wash and dry large pieces of lettuce. Show them how to peel their carrots. Cut off the ends of the carrots for the children. Each child will need a carrot and piece of lettuce for a zooloo. Demonstrate wrapping the carrot in a "blanket" of lettuce, securing it with a toothpick. Ask each group of three to form a letter **Z** with their zooloos. You may want to collect the toothpicks before allowing the children to eat the snacks. These are a fun snack to take on a walk to eat along the way!

Other taste experiences for letter **Z**: zucchini and zwieback.

SONGS AND POEMS

Song: "Zip-a-Zee-Zoo-Zah"

(tune of "Zip-a-Dee-Doo-Dah")

Zip-a-zee-zoo-zah, zip-a-zee-zay.
Zing, zing, zing, it's a letter **Z** day!
Zip-a-zee-zoo-zah, zip-a-zee-zay.
Zip-a-zee-zoo-zah, happy **Z** day! *(for zip, jump up; clap the beat on the rest of the song; sing with spirit)*

Poem: "My Zipper Suit"

My zipper suit is bunny brown.
The top zips up *(motion with one hand from stomach to chin)*
The legs zip down. *(motion with one hand downward along leg)*
My Grandma brought it from out of town.
Zip it up and zip it down, *(repeat other motions)*
And then go out to play!

ZANY ZEBRA

Teacher Directions: Cut out the circles. Put them face down in a box decorated as a cage. You can make more than one set.

Student Directions: Sit together in a circle. Take turns picking up a circle card. If you can name the number on the circle, you can keep it. If not, put it back. If you get a happy zebra, take another turn. If you get a sad zebra, put one of your circles back. Have a zany time!

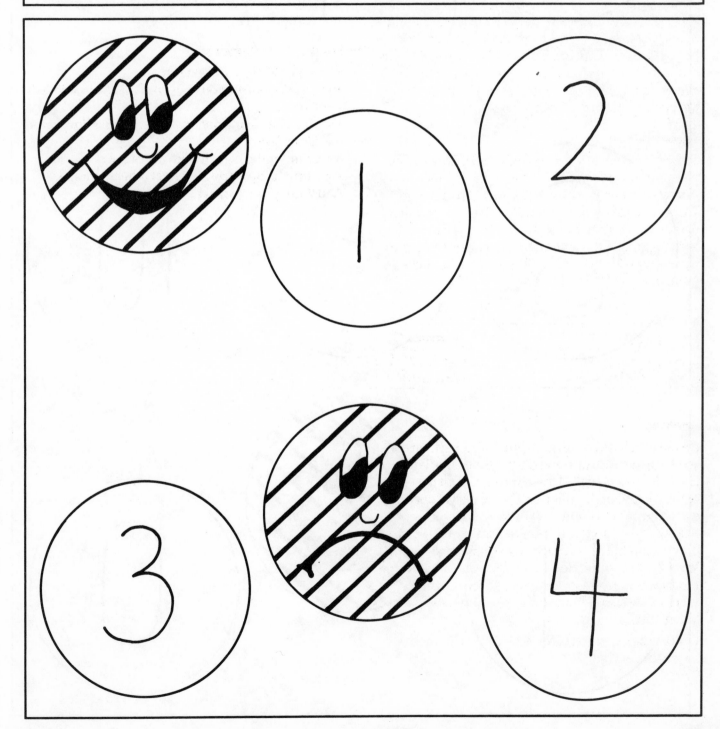